AMERICAN POLITICS

Also by Milton Meltzer

Poverty in America

Starting from Home: A Writer's Beginnings

Rescue:
The Story of How Gentiles Saved Jews in the Holocaust

Never to Forget: The Jews of the Holocaust

Benjamin Franklin: The New American

George Washington and the Birth of Our Nation

The American Revolutionaries:
A History in Their Own Words, 1750–1800

Mark Twain: A Writer's Life

Langston Hughes: A Biography

The Landscape of Memory

Ain't Gonna Study War No More:
The Story of America's Peace Seekers

The Black Americans: A History in Their Own Words

The Jewish Americans: A History in Their Own Words

The Chinese Americans

The Hispanic Americans

All Times, All Peoples: A World History of Slavery

AMERICAN POLITICS

HOW IT REALLY WORKS

★BY★

Milton Meltzer

★ILLUSTRATIONS BY★

David Small

Morrow Junior Books

New York

For Julia and Dwight Whitney

Inquiries should be addressed to
William Morrow and Company, Inc.,
105 Madison Avenue,
New York, NY 10016.
Printed in the United States of America.
1 2 3 4 5 6 7 8 9 10
Library of Congress Cataloging-in-Publication Data
Meltzer, Milton.
American politics.
Bibliography: p.
Includes index.
1. United States—Politics and government—Juvenile
literature.   I. Title.
JK40.M45   1989   320.473   88-26635
ISBN 0-688-07494-4

CONTENTS

1. The Art of Politics   1
2. Struggle and Compromise   9
3. It Began in Revolution   21
4. The Great Election Show   32
5. Hi-Tech Campaigning   43
6. Why So Few Voters at the Polls?   52
7. Republicans, Democrats, and Who Else?   61
8. Presidents: They Come in All Kinds   68
9. What Congress Does or Fails to Do   80
10. The Last Word on the Law   97
11. Lobbyists and Those They Serve   107
12. Bureaucrats and Whistle-Blowers   118
13. Muckrakers and Millionaires   128
14. The Cost of Corruption   142
15. To Make a Difference   152
    A Note on Sources   170
    Bibliography   175
    Index   179

1

THE ART
OF POLITICS

Say "politics" and many people wrinkle their nose in disgust. It has come to be a dirty word in the popular vocabulary. When promotions are planned on the campus or in the corporation, the cynic mutters, "You've got to know how to play politics to get yours." And it's true. For politics is something we all do when trying to get what we want in a world of limited resources.

A certain amount of politics is practiced in just about every situation involving groups of people, small or large. It happens in the tenants committee, the trade union, the business office, the social agency, the school faculty, the law firm, the women's group, the housing committee, a thousand other places.

Most commonly we think of politics in connection with government, with the art of organizing, regulating, and administering the affairs of the state. This book will deal with politics in that realm. But much of what it will say about politics in government applies to many of the other situations in life where people meet to discuss and negotiate their differences.

Still, you say, I can do without politics. But can you? Like it or not, politics is a powerful force determining the conditions of life. You may choose to stay out of the game, glad to avoid the stink, the noise, the fakery. But you can't escape its effects. For politics shapes the decisions made by governments—federal, state, or local— and these decisions touch almost every aspect of your daily life: education, business, jobs, pollution, the environment, communications, taxation, budgets, housing, health, transportation, civil rights, justice, war. . . . The list is unlimited. All these are affected by policy decisions, decisions that benefit some groups of people, hurt others. They impose costs that are heavier for some to bear, lighter for others. When you think about it, you realize that a great many political decisions influence economic matters. A government's budget and its taxing and spending policies are at the heart of politics. They bear directly upon the quality of life every citizen experiences.

So from the point of view of your own immediate interests, it is important to know something about politics: what it is and how it really works. Who governs your life and how do they do it? Our hopes and fears are bound up with the answers.

Politics is first of all an activity. It is not a thing, like a rock, something that's simply there. Politics arises in societies made up of different groups, with different interests and traditions. These groups, existing together, on the same territory, or in the same governmental unit, have rival interests that make a common government essential if there is to be any order. But the problem of making order has more than one solution. A tyrant may rise to rule in his or her own interest. Or one group, an oligarchy, may take control in the interest of its own members. The method of rule of tyrants and oligarchies is simply to force, by whatever means necessary, the subordination of all other groups to themselves.

Democratic politics applies a different kind of solution to the problem of governing. People who support the political method of rule accept the fact that different groups have conflicting interests. Unlike tyrants or oligarchies, people who support the political method of rule listen to all the groups, work out compromises among them, and accord each group a legal position, a sense of security, and the freedom to speak openly for its needs. Ideally, all these groups contribute to the maintenance of order. They do this by infinitely varied means, depending upon the strength or weakness of competing interests. It is never a perfect process of reconciling differences. But it is radically different, and better, most would agree, than tyranny, a junta, a dictatorship, or totalitarian rule, whether of the right or the left.

Of course, even in tyrannical regimes there are elements of what some term politics. These are confined, however, to struggles for power within a single party or between two powerful figures seeking a monopoly of power. With complete victory, the faction or individual contending for power suppresses the losers and then acts alone to rule the state. In such unfree regimes, the winner often achieves his or her goal only by violence, and the loser may pay in blood.

So politics can be seen as the activity by which different interests within a governing unit work out compromises in proportion to their influence. Politics thus ensures a reasonable amount of stability and order. Nothing is final about any compromise reached. Compromise simply serves some purpose at the time it is made and allows government to carry on. That political compromise maintains order is a fact most people value, especially if they are given some choice in the matter. Politics might be compared to a marketplace where social demands are settled by negotiation. A bargain is struck among contending forces. There is, of course, no assurance that a just price has been paid.

Does politics as defined here mean that everyone shares some idea of the "common good" or "public interest"? Not at all. The various groups that constitute the community, as already suggested, have conflicting interests or needs. They hold together under one government because they do share an interest in plain survival as a community. By practicing politics, they may succeed in doing that. They don't have to agree on fundamentals, or on some intangible spiritual concern, to get on with practicing politics. Politics enables us to survive and to avoid an unacceptable amount of coercion. Through politics we can strive to adapt to continual social, economic, and technological change as we seek to enjoy the rich variety of a civilized society.

Any honest look at politics has to take account of its abuses. There are all too many people who live for power

and profit and who use politics solely for those ends. But to criticize their operations is not to attack politics itself. If in the course of this book abuses are exposed, the aim is to help rid ourselves of such abuses. We dream of a society free of poverty, racism, sexism, and exploitation in any form. Those who hold to that dream want to use the art of politics to see justice fulfilled.

Constant talk of conflicts within the community makes politics sound like some kind of warfare. So it is, in one sense, but without conquest as the goal. The ideas and the views of one group may clash with those of another group. Nevertheless, through politics the differences are brought into the open; they are discussed and debated. The private agendas of some groups may be concealed by unscrupulous politicians. But democracy, the form of government we are talking about, doesn't guarantee us a fair and wise government. Its aim is to give people a voice in the management of their own affairs. Through political action, through the bargaining process, people reach an accommodation. Each group may not get its first choice, but when it finds that to be the case, the group settles for its second or third choice.

That politics is a mixture of self-interest and the public interest was clear to young Benjamin Franklin. Back in 1731, when he was twenty-five, he jotted down some observations on what he had learned about politics from using his eyes and from reading history:

• That the great affairs of the world, the wars, revolutions, etc., are carried on and effected by parties.
• That the view of these parties is their present general interest, or what they take to be such.

- That the different views of these different parties occasion all confusion.
- That while a party is carrying on a general design, each man has his particular private interest in view.
- That as soon as a party has gained its general point, each member becomes intent upon his particular interest; which thwarting others, breaks that party into divisions, and occasions more confusion.
- That few in public affairs act from a mere view of the good of their country, whatever they may pretend; and, though their actings bring real good to their country, yet men primarily considered that their own and their country's interest was united, and did not act from a principle of benevolence.
- That fewer still, in public affairs, act with a view to the good of mankind.

On November 8, 1988, a few days before this book went on press, the election of America's forty-first president took place. Although not enough time has passed for a long perspective, it is possible to make some observations. And they clearly reflect what Franklin had to say about politics. There was a mixture of self-interest and the public interest, but this time the drive to win overwhelmed concern for the public good.

George Bush, the Republican party candidate, defeated Michael Dukakis, his Democratic opponent, by the kind of high-tech campaigning described later in these pages. Advertising and television experts packaged their campaigns to sell the candidates like any other product. Well-rehearsed little stunts were staged every day for a few seconds of managed impact on nightly television. Images and symbols became far more important than information. The mudslinging and the failure to talk about the real issues disgusted so many that the voter turnout was the lowest in history.

One news analyst, James Reston, blamed the Republicans for a "cheap-shot" campaign of "calculated misrepresentation" of Dukakis and called Bush's "win-at-any-cost hucksters . . . a disgrace to the democratic process."

In this brand of politicking, the distinction between the real and the unreal, between news and entertainment, is deliberatley lost. Showmanship makes false promises and raises false fears. Such campaigns are not about the issues of the world we live in but about the world as the campaign managers want us to see it.

The various groups that make up the American public do have conflicting interests and needs, as this book demonstrates. But the one interest they all share is in survival as a community. The ability of citizens in a democracy to discuss their problems freely and resolve them by political compromise is threatened by the kind of campaigning witnessed in 1988. A civilized election would educate voters about the issues that need to be decided, not treat them like fools that can be manipulated by fear and falsehoods.

An uncritical media, both print and electronic, is much to blame for not giving serious coverage to the issues. And as this book points out, voters are not blameless, either. Politicians look at results. If low, ugly, and evasive campaigning wins elections, they will keep doing it. Campaigns can improve, but only if voters are more demanding of the candidates and show that a corrupted political process does not work.

2

STRUGGLE
AND
COMPROMISE

It was Franklin's hardheaded view of politics in the real world that moved the Founding Fathers when they wrote our Constitution in 1787. The fifty-five delegates from the sovereign states came together in Philadelphia to work out how the young nation would be governed. During the Revolution each state had insisted on the right to rule itself and refused to surrender its sovereignty to the Continental Congress. Congress continued to have little power under the Articles of Confederation, ratified in 1781. The Congress proved to be so weak that the states saw a strong central government was badly needed to assure order by coordinating their conflicting interests.

What were the interests of the Framers of the Constitution of the United States? The men who played the dominant role in shaping the new government were rich and wellborn—successful planters, lawyers, merchants.

Many were linked by kinship and marriage and by common service in the Continental Congress, the military, and the colonial governments. There was no class of nobles in the thirteen states, but these were "gentlemen" who were proud of what they owned and had no desire to give it up. Many lived in fine mansions on great estates. Their families had profited for generations from huge land grants made by the Crown. Fewer than a dozen families owned three-quarters of the acreage in the colony of New York in 1700. By 1760, most of the commerce, banking, mining, and manufacturing and much of the land on the eastern seaboard was in the hands of fewer than 500 men.

But the great majority of the Americans owned little or nothing and knew no such luxury. They worked on the land as freeholders, tenants, or indentured laborers. The poor were in the cities too, working long hours as craftspeople, servants, or laborers. Lack of property severely limited a man's rights. In most of the states men had to own so much property to vote that about a third of the white males were disfranchised. Women did not have the political right to vote. The exception was in New Jersey from the 1780s until 1807, when that right was taken away. To qualify as a candidate for public office men had to own even more property, so much that most voters could never get on the ballot. This meant that the well-to-do men took all the important offices. Women could not hold public office.

The outcome of these class differences was pretty much what Adam Smith, the pioneer economist, observed it to be. Government, he said, is "instituted for the defense of

the rich against the poor" and "grows up with the acquisition of valuable property."

When the delegates to the Constitutional Convention met at Philadelphia that summer of 1787, they were deeply troubled by the rebellious spirit demonstrated by the poor farmers and villagers. Land seizures by the poor and food riots had often occurred in about every colony or state. Only a few months before, Shays's Rebellion had broken out in western Massachusetts. The soldiers, ragged and penniless at the end of the Revolutionary War, had headed home without the pay long overdue them. Congress, itself without funds, had asked the states to pay the wages owed the soldiers, but many of the states failed to act. Back home, the veterans found themselves deeply in debt, mainly to the merchants. Fearing the courts would foreclose on their farms, a force of 1,500 men led by Captain Daniel Shays descended on the courts to prevent them from sitting. The protestors broke into jails and freed prisoners held for debt. The panicky governor sent out 4,000 troops to prevent Shays's attack upon a U.S. arsenal. The rebels were defeated in a skirmish.

Shays's Rebellion made the wealthy class fear that state governments might be taken over directly by the people who were seeking justice. The wealthy wanted a constitution that would guarantee order and protect their propertied interests. So at Philadelphia they put aside the old Articles of Confederation and wrote a completely new constitution. The Framers were not idealists dreaming up plans for a utopian government. They were soldiers, lawyers, businessmen, planters, merchants, legislators—men experienced in the harsh ways of the marketplaces, legislatures, battlefields. They had themselves struggled to win or to keep power and wealth. They knew human passions. Shays's Rebellion had intensified their fear of the propertyless majority. Persons of property believed they were best qualified to control the government of the United States. They wanted to check what they called "the levelling impulse" of the poor. James Madison, a key delegate, wrote that the great object of the Constitutional Convention was "to secure the public good and private rights against such a faction and at the same time preserve the spirit and form of popular government. . . ."

At Philadelphia there were no illusions about changing the nature of human beings to fit some ideal system. Yet from their experience of life and their reading of history, the delegates believed a form of self-government was best. Government by the consent of the governed. With Benjamin Franklin, the oldest among them, they agreed that by their very nature, people act on self-interest. So a democracy must be strong enough to curb any tendency to greed and corruption. However, since strong government is itself a threat to liberty, effective limits must be set upon governmental authority.

Many of the delegates saw the threat to liberty as a threat to their right to property. Madison observed that "the most common and durable source of factions has been the various and unequal distribution of property. Those who hold and those who are without property have ever formed distinct interests in society." So "the first object of government" is "the protection of different and unequal faculties of acquiring property." From that point of view, one delegate, Elbridge Gerry, called democracy "the worst of all political evils." Like Madison, he feared "the danger of the levelling spirit." Another delegate, Roger Sherman, told the Constitutional Convention that "the people should have as little to do as may be about the Government." And Alexander Hamilton (later secretary of the treasury under Washington) asserted that "all communities divide themselves into the few and the many. The first are the rich and the well-born, the other the mass of the people. . . . The people are turbulent and changing; they seldom judge or determine right."

On questions of property, the Constitutional Convention came to ready agreement. There were no delegates to speak for the poor and propertyless. The voice of the have-nots was silent, except as echoes of Shays reached into the hall. Under Article 1, Section 8, of the Constitution, the federal government was given the power to regulate commerce and protect property, with many provisions to that end spelled out carefully. While congressional action was limited to powers specially delegated to it by the Constitution, one clause said that Congress could make any laws deemed "necessary and proper" to carry out its delegated powers. That "implied power" clause, as time went on, was interpreted to permit extensive intervention in the private economy by the federal government.

Although most delegates were upper-class people, still there were serious differences among them. The smaller states were jealous of the larger; the northerners and southerners distrusted one another; commercial interests ran against agricultural interests. But slowly, painfully, the delegates worked their way to reconciliation of their differences. They found they had to compromise if they were to achieve anything meaningful and lasting.

One major issue was the division of power: between the central government and the states, and between states with large populations and states with small populations. The deadlock between the bigger and smaller states was broken by giving something to both. There would be two chambers of Congress. In the lower house, the House of Representatives, representation would be on the basis of population, pleasing the larger states. In the upper house, the Senate, the smaller and larger states got equal representation: two members elected for each state no matter what their population. This pleased the smaller states.

The differences between the agricultural South and the commercial North were reconciled by another major compromise. On the one hand, Congress was given the right to regulate trade, which pleased the northern shipping and commercial interests. On the other hand, Congress was forbidden to enact duties on exports. That pleased the agricultural South, which depended on exports for its income.

Slavery, the dominant issue between North and South, was dealt with in still another compromise. It did not take up much time, for this was a question of protection of property interests, and agreement was reached without much debate. The delegates permitted slavery to remain legal to keep the lower South, where it was important for the production of major crops, in the Union. Slaves were to be counted at three-fifths of their number as a basis for representation in Congress. That pleased the North, which did not want the many southern slaves counted in the same proportion as free people for representation purposes. The African slave trade could not be interfered with for another twenty years, and the states were required to return fugitive slaves to their owners. Thus slavery was propped up as the price for getting southern support for the new centralized federal government.

The delegates then went on to establish an executive branch and a judiciary. A president, chosen by a majority of electors from each of the states, would head the executive, with a veto over acts of Congress that only a two-thirds majority of both houses could override. The president's functions were spelled out. There would be an independent federal judiciary with judges appointed for life. A Supreme Court would have the highest judicial power. Its justices would be appointed by the president subject to the advice and consent of the Senate.

A system of separation of powers was agreed upon, with each branch—the legislative, the executive, and the judicial—having different powers. The Congress would pass the laws, the president would see that they were carried out, and the Supreme Court would resolve disputes. The aim was to prevent concentration of power in any branch, thus blocking the growth of tyranny.

But what if one of the branches should try to cripple or destroy the others? Against that possibility the Convention devised what we call the system of checks and balances. It guaranteed each branch the power to check both of the others' actions. The president could veto the laws of Congress. The Senate could disapprove the president's treaties and refuse office to people the president selected. The president could appoint judges, but those judges could declare unlawful certain acts of the president and his assistants. Congress would have certain powers, but the Supreme Court could decide when Congress went beyond its proper authority.

Majority rule was a fundamental principle the Convention guaranteed in the Constitution. The House of Representatives would be elected by majority vote of those allowed to vote, and would pass laws only when a majority of both houses agreed. The Senate was elected by the state legislatures. Not until the Seventeenth Amendment (1913) were senators elected directly by the people. Elections would be held often so that the people could vote on whether they liked or disapproved of what candidates stood for or did.

Yet rule by majority can be oppressive if it acts against a disliked or despised minority. So the Constitution must ensure that a minority's rights can't be violated or ignored just because a majority wants to. With the passage of the Bill of Rights, the Constitution would guarantee certain unalienable rights to some. It was considered unwise to give the majority of adults who were called "dependent" people—women, slaves, men without property—the same rights as others. To shield judges from pressure, they would hold office for life. Then judges need not fear a majority's anger when they protected the rights of an unpopular minority.

As realists, the delegates knew they were not perfect; they knew their Constitution could not be so perfect as to meet the changing needs of all the generations to come.

If mistakes are human, then correcting them must be made possible; the Framers opened the Constitution to change by spelling out an amendment procedure.

As the newly drafted Constitution circulated in the states for ratification, a powerful swell of protest rose. Where was a Bill of Rights? How could the Convention have ignored the ancient British tradition of the people's rights, going back to the Magna Carta of 1215? The colonial Americans had often pointed to those rights when they protested the arbitrary acts of British officials. That was why most states had put a Bill of Rights into their own constitutions. But at Philadelphia the delegates had paid more attention to the rights of property than to the rights of persons. They meant to protect freedom to invest, to trade, to accumulate wealth, and to shield it against invasion by any leveling faction. When George Mason of Virginia had asked for a committee to draft a Bill of Rights, the other delegates discussed it only briefly and then all voted against it. True, there were scattered provisions of some important liberties in the draft, but back home the people felt the Constitution didn't go far enough. Jefferson argued that a Bill of Rights "is what the people are entitled to against every government on earth . . . and what no just government should refuse."

Devoid of a Bill of Rights, the Constitution had a hard time making its way to adoption. In many states it was at first opposed by majorities. But the backers of the draft had the money, the organization, and the press to push through a ratification campaign. Some citizens openly resented it. Said one man in Massachusetts:

These lawyers, and men of learning, and moneyed men, that talk so finely, and gloss over matters so smoothly, to make us, poor illiterate people, swallow down the pill, expect to get into Congress themselves; they expect to be the managers of this Constitution, and get all the power and all the money into their own hands, and then they will swallow up all us little folks, like the great leviathan.

It's worth noting that the Constitution was not adopted by popular vote. Ratification was done by state conventions whose delegates came mostly from the same well-off class as the Founding Fathers.

By the middle of 1787, nine states had ratified the Constitution, putting it into effect. When the first Congress under the new Constitution met in 1789, a Bill of Rights was adopted in the form of a number of amendments. It was not until 1791, however, that the states ratified ten of them. The Bill of Rights consists of these first ten amendments to the Constitution. They guarantee freedoms for the individual that no government can take away.

Whatever may be its weaknesses, the Constitution marked a great gain for democracy. A written constitution with limited powers was far superior to the autocratic forms of government much of the world suffered under. To hold federal office, no citizen need own a certain amount of property. This was different from law in England or in many of the states. Public officials would be paid for their services, which meant a man didn't have to be rich to afford the time required for public office. From the president on down, federal officeholders were elected for a limited term, cutting off any lifetime lock on office. No matter what a candidate's religion, he was eligible for any office or public trust in the United States. No longer could Roman Catholics or Jews be barred from office.

Such provisions as these, plus the direct election of the House of Representatives and the adoption of the Bill of Rights, helped the new government win popular support.

Yes, the Framers were moneyed men who saw to it that their interests were protected under the new Constitution. But that did not mean they did not also want to build a strong democratic republic. They believed that what was good for themselves was in the long run good for the nation too. Like most people, as Franklin said, their universal values and their self-interest ran together. They were made up of contradictions, like most of us. Didn't Jefferson declare that "all men are created free and equal" at the same time that he owned slaves?

The creation of the Constitution was itself a demonstration of the art of politics. Groups got whatever they could to satisfy their interests, and gave in whenever pressure from other groups obliged them to. It was an example of struggle and compromise that would recur again and again as decisions affecting our everyday lives would be made by government.

3

IT BEGAN
IN REVOLUTION

The American republic has been running for over 200 years under the Constitution adopted in 1787. How does it work? What forces shape political life? What do people get out of it?

Look back to the Continental Congress declaring American independence. It pronounced new principles of government:

We hold these truths to be self-evident, that all men are created equal, that they are endowed by their Creator with certain unalienable rights, that among these are Life, Liberty, and the pursuit of Happiness. That to secure these rights, Governments are instituted among Men, deriving their just powers from the consent of the governed.

Many social studies textbooks give us a glowing portrait of those brave and wise men who pledged their lives,

their fortunes, and their sacred honor to establish and
defend the Declaration's great principles. Then they go
on to describe the structure of government. A somewhat
idealized picture of American politics and government
usually emerges. It goes something like this:

The people who founded the nation had the good of
everyone at heart. They wrote a Constitution to establish
a democracy (though nowhere in it does that word occur)
and prevent abuses of power. Under it, people elect a
president and Congress to serve their needs. In our republic, citizens do not have a direct voice in government,
but express their will through a Congress and a president
they elect periodically. These officials make the decisions.
Their powers are checked by the balanced form of government and by the fact that they must satisfy the voters
in order to remain in office. Decisions of government are
made by majority vote, with provision for the protection
of minority rights.

Since we are a large nation of diverse peoples and
interests—many ethnic, racial, social, economic, and re-
gional groups—public officials face competing demands.
It makes conflict inevitable. Government's job is to me-
diate these varying demands, with the public benefit always in mind. The result is generally a compromise, with
no group getting its way completely. Yet every group is
heard as compromise is reached. No group rules the roost.
On the whole, the system operates with fairly good participation by the society at large. It has given us a free
and prosperous United States, the most powerful nation
in the world.

But is that the way things really are? Or is it only the

way we wish things were? The best way to determine that is to look at what actually happens. What do citizens want, and what do politicians do? Who gets what, and why? Political scientists study just such questions in the universities and the think tanks. People who served in government—in the White House, the Congress, the courts, the thousands of agencies and bureaus—tell their version of what goes on in autobiographies, memoirs, interviews, articles, letters, and collections of their personal and public papers. Some of these records are honest, some distort the truth, some are mixed. Then there is the work of historians and biographers and journalists who have written countless books on politics and politicians.

A look at the political system requires examination of all the branches of government and the ways they operate. Politics includes political parties, elections, laws, lobbyists, and interest or pressure groups. They're all tied together. Public policy is the outcome of their interaction. This book can't go into a detailed analysis of every facet of the system. That would be an encyclopedic task. Its aim is simply to provide a brief and general picture, to suggest what some experts have learned, and to raise some questions worth thinking about.

In the first chapter we discussed the nature of politics. It comes down to a power struggle over goods, settled by negotiation. But it's also the process of working out agreement on what the goods are. Groups differ over such questions as free trade, inflation, taxation, welfare, unemployment, wages, social security. Politics often begins with the effort to decide what's important, what's worth negotiation: Is this an issue that demands settlement through political action? Just to get the matter on the table obliges legislators to work together.

Power is a word used often when talking politics. One writer defines it as "the ability to get what one wants, either by having one's interests prevail in conflicts with others or by preventing others from raising conflicting demands." The powerful people have the strength to get others to do what the powerful wish. They have the resources for such control: the organization, the media, the technology, the skills, the jobs, the goods and services people hope for—and the money that makes it all possible.

Politics sometimes starts with head-on confrontation. In the 1950s and 1960s, after experiencing generations of neglect or hostility, black Americans conducted campaigns of civil disobedience. They forced the politicians to recognize that their condition needed action. Finally, political leaders put civil rights on the agenda and started to negotiate over what legislation would satisfy black demands.

The same course was taken by the trade unions in the 1930s when they organized mass strikes in basic industries to force employers to the bargaining table.

So at bottom, politics is agreement over what to negotiate about and how to do the bargaining. When politicians refuse to believe that some vital questions can be negotiated, they risk the alternative: revolution or civil war. An awareness of, a sensitivity to, the public interest is what keeps the political game going. A rigid posture can cripple the political process. The politics of a democracy requires common recognition of the need for alliances, for compromise, even for retreat.

If the new government of the United States was to succeed, everyone agreed that no one but George Washington must preside over its launching. Called "our adored leader," he was unanimously elected president of the United States. No political parties existed at the time; the Constitution made no provision for them. The Founding Fathers distrusted parties and called them factions. It's a word that implies fringe groups out to control the rest of the community. To set up parties would invite corruption, the Framers thought. They believed citizens would vote for candidates without party labels, men who would reach agreement on what was good for the entire nation. The legislators would take full responsibility for making decisions.

But hardly was the Constitution ratified when political parties began to form. People who knew what they wanted saw that a strong federal government would make important decisions affecting the interests of every group for good or bad. Politics mattered, then, and people with like interests ought to join in parties to influence the decisions of government in their favor.

The dominant figures in Washington's cabinet were Alexander Hamilton, who was secretary of the treasury, and Thomas Jefferson, who was secretary of state. They took leadership in the political struggle over whose interests the government would serve. Hamilton spoke for the Federalists, the well-to-do conservatives; he wanted to put the government on a sound financial basis. His measures favored the moneyed seaboard class, while leaving the agricultural South pretty much to shift for itself. The young financial wizard drove straight toward his goal, indifferent to popular protest.

Jefferson led the anti-Federalists, the class of southern planters and small farmers of all regions who saw the government was helping business by generous credit while giving themselves no relief from debt and taxation. They felt threatened by the power of the "ins," the Federalist party.

Jefferson thought Hamilton was a monarchist at heart, a dangerous reactionary, opposed to political or social change. Jefferson was suspicious of the business class and opposed monopoly and special favors granted to the Hamilton establishment. The Virginian dreamed of an American arcadia based on a nation of farmers. He feared the rise of cities and mistrusted the people who worked in them. He wanted to keep government small and society simple.

The two contending parties treated each other as bitter enemies. *We're* the saints, each said; *they're* the devils. Of course it was true of neither. Both parties quickly came to use the slogans, catchphrases, and stereotypes that have characterized political strife ever since. Neither party, in those early years, drew broad public participation. The direction of party policy was in the hands of only a few people, both on the state and national levels.

Washington was chosen unanimously for a second term. When he stepped down, the new political parties took over. Very soon it became clear that a two-party system would dominate American politics. The names of the par-

ties would change from time to time, and sometimes a new party would arise, made up of various interest groups so dissatisfied with the way things were that they wanted a new structure to represent them. The Democratic party was created by Andrew Jackson's supporters, who elected him to the presidency in 1828. The Republican party was born in 1854 out of the slavery issue, and six years later had its candidate, Abraham Lincoln, elected president. These parties have continued right up to today.

The Republicans are the rare example of a third party that managed to become one of the two major parties. Other third parties have sprung to life out of some very specific felt need. Some feared Masonry, some wanted paper currency, some tried to end drinking. Such parties secured broad support for a time, perhaps won office on local and state levels or even in the Congress, but then faded away. A quick glance at some of these parties and the first years they ran presidential candidates shows how frequently third parties have occurred. Most of them died quickly:

Independent-Republican, 1808
Anti-Masonic, 1832
Liberty, 1844
Free Soil, 1848
American, 1856
Constitutional Union, 1860
Greenback-Labor, 1880
Prohibition, 1884
Union Labor, 1888
People's, 1892
Populist, 1900
Socialist, 1904

Progressive, 1912
Farmer Labor, 1920
Union, 1936
States' Rights, 1948
Progressive, 1948
American Independent, 1968
Libertarian, 1980

Party labels can be misleading. You have to examine the policy and program beneath the labels to understand what a party stands for. The Republican party of today, like the rival Democratic party, has shifted in program, strategy, and appeal in the continuous process of adapting to social and economic change. Parties try to tune in to what people want, what they will do, and what they will stand for, in order to gain the majority support needed to win power and hold it. The political scientist V. O. Key noted that both parties "change at about the same rate and generally in the same direction. Their policies are the policies of a capitalist society modified as recurring internal crises demand."

The two parties may have somewhat different general tendencies, but both strive for the support of a cross section of the population. That brings them to take a stance somewhere in the middle on most issues. Many political analysts think the system is a success because the differences between the two parties have been so small. The losers in an election are willing to accept the outcome, and the winners don't want to push their advantage so far that they infuriate the losers. Thus both parties continually adapt themselves to what they perceive as the needs of the country.

Within parties there exists the same need to compromise conflicting interests as within the national government. Many groups gather under a party's banner;
inevitably they don't agree on every issue or tactic. So
politics operates inside the party, too. Achieving compromise is not a neat, clean-cut affair. It's a messy business: give, take, push, shove, pull, haul, drag, threaten,
promise. All in the hope of keeping the party together
and moving forward. Or just holding its own. If righteous
party leaders insist on having their own way, they are
likely to lose support. People want some choice, some
chance to contribute to solutions. They resent that iron-
bound certainty which permits no disagreement.

If you find total agreement within a political community—local, state, federal—you can be sure it happened only by force or fraud. In a free society, politics
doesn't operate on dogma or by any set of fixed beliefs.
There is always change, coming out of the very essence
of political activity. But, you may say, you're tired of the
constant bickering and wrangling and criticizing and the
slow coming to decisions. Can't we do without this continual tension on the political scene? It's not possible. A
society as diverse as ours is packed with rival groups,
classes, interests, and attitudes, and that diversity is the
root of politics. Nothing can remove the tensions produced by conflicting needs and claims. Politics is the way
we handle those differences, so that society can maintain
the degree of unity it needs to survive. There isn't any
magic, any mass therapy that could cure those tensions.
A totalitarian regime might succeed in masking them. But

the tensions would exist underneath, and some day might force themselves to the surface—as they did not long ago in Portugal, Spain, Argentina, and Greece, where fascist rulers or military juntas finally lost power through popular upheaval.

4

THE GREAT ELECTION SHOW

"The greatest show on earth!"

That's what our national elections are often called. The ballyhoo and hoopla reach into the home every evening on the TV screen. Now, no longer a seasonal event, it stretches out for years. No sooner is a candidate safely in office than he or she begins running for the next term. Tiresome and boring as it sometimes gets to be, the popular election of those who govern is central to the political system.

But is it more than just a show? Does it give us solid discussion of the real issues or just a horse race? The media focus on questions such as, who's going to run? Is the candidate handsome or dumpy, square or sharp, stiff or relaxed, dull or witty, prim or sexy? As the race gets going, the questions become who's ahead, who's slipping, who's taking this primary, who's out front for the nomination, who'll win the election?

How often is it asked, What do you, the candidate, stand for? What are your ideas? What is your approach to the country's problems? What program of action do you propose? The great election show no longer pays attention to these kinds of questions. It can, and once it did. Look back to the Lincoln-Douglas debates of 1858, when the two men from Illinois were running for the U.S. Senate. Seven times they shared platforms across the state to debate the slavery issue that was dividing the country. They faced the issues squarely, and the nation's newspapers reprinted their words, giving the citizens the chance to weigh the merits of each position and make up their own mind. It was an exercise in true democracy that in recent times we rarely, if ever, witness.

From time to time people grow tired of what they see as a "political circus." In recent years more citizens than ever have felt that way. They don't think much of the quality of the candidates, and see little difference among them. They don't hear real issues debated and resent the mudslinging. They wonder if these endless primaries do any good. They are appalled by the huge sums of money shoveled into campaigns. Sure, politics is important, but is this trivial stuff the real thing?

Election campaigns used to be run by political machines dominated by professional leaders. The machines handed out small favors in their districts to win the votes of deprived groups—especially workers and immigrants in the cities. The politicians gave big favors to railroad magnates, land speculators, public utilities, building contractors, banks, and of course, to themselves. In the end, the poor paid for the few favors they got: taxation went easy on the rich and hard on the poor. The upper classes got not only large rewards for supporting the machine but the comfort of knowing the machine would do just enough for the mass of voters to keep them from upsetting the apple cart.

The power of those old-time political bosses has dwindled. Among the last of the "back room Caesars" was Richard J. Daley of Chicago, who died in 1976. The shadow of the boss may still fall over a few places, but now such influence rarely reaches above the local level. Political workers don't need to carry leaflets into the neighborhood or ring doorbells to spread the message. When many states adopted the direct primary, it meant candidates could try for nomination through the ballot box. They didn't have to make a deal with a political boss to get on the ticket. Many of the party machines fell apart. They may still keep the office open, but few walk in.

Today most candidates, while running on a party ticket, get along without the party machine except for help in fund-raising. They hire their own professional consultants who tell them what to wear, how to look, where to go, and what to say, when. Besides money fed them by the party, the fund-raising experts seek out the big contributors to pay for the candidates' personal staff, the traveling, and the expensive media campaign.

Does the lesser role of the party organizations mean greater independence for the candidate? Surely we'd expect a richer variety of political views, a freer and broader range of ideas and programs. But no. The result has been all the less attention to important issues and all the more care given to cultivating an appealing image. The candidates are less accountable to both the party and the public. They seem to compete to be more like one another rather than different. They offer the citizens little choice of any substance.

The reason? Money. It's a powerful force in the corruption of the democratic process. In the 1980s, Elizabeth Drew, the veteran Washington correspondent, made a thorough study of its role. Her findings are based upon close observation over the past twenty-five years and upon interviews with people at the heart of the political system. As running for office on any level, from the cities and states through Congress and the White House, has become ever more costly, the raising of funds to pay for the campaigns, she says, has driven the politicians into a new form of political corruption. Even those who want to avoid this corruption find it hard to do so.

The pressure is double: to raise big money for themselves and to prevent big money from being spent against them. So heavy is that pressure, it affects the way politicians do their job more than it ever did. The result is that lobbyists and lawyers who want to shape public policies to benefit their clients have acquired finely honed skills in dealing with politicians. Both the legislative process and the legislative product, Drew says, are distorted by this. It has brought us far from the way representative government is supposed to work.

If you stop to think about it, it's not hard to understand

how this fund raising works. To get into office the candidate has to solicit or accept money from those who have plenty of it. That means behaving in office the way your big contributors will like. Yes, there are federal laws setting limits on contributions to congressional and presidential campaigns. But despite these, reports Drew, "great rivers of private money, much of it untraceable, still flow into them." To the big contributors and fund-raisers go ambassadorships, cabinet posts, and other high positions.

One lobbyist told Drew:

The key thing is what all this is doing to the way we govern ourselves. I think we are reaching the point where legislators make decisions only after thinking about what this means in terms of the money that will come to them or go to their opponents. . . . Everyone on Capitol Hill knows that cash is swapped for legislation or regulatory rulings.

Drew points out that the effect of money on lawmaking can take several forms. Some of them seem to contradict one another (but not really), while others are hidden from view:

Because of the need for money or the fear of a well-financed opponent, a member of Congress might vote a certain way on a piece of legislation, or might try to avoid a vote on the matter, or might even forestall congressional consideration of it altogether. The effect might be in some action in a subcommittee, or some message to a colleague, that does not come to light. Legislation that in the earlier years might not have ever been seriously considered but has the backing of a particularly well-financed interest group can go whizzing through Congress. Other legislation, often involving important issues, can be so caught in the tangle of competing interests that Congress is paralyzed.

Standing on the sidelines, as most of us do, we can grasp one fact: the big, monied interests have a huge head start over the rest of us. Money talks so loud that the voice of the people is often drowned out. This doesn't mean that interest groups shouldn't try to shape public policy. They always have, from the first Congress on, and it's natural. Lawmakers are elected to speak for the people they represent. It's nonsense to think that they are supposed to be "above" pressure groups. To say that legislators would do better in their jobs if they didn't have to listen to constituent groups is like saying democracy would be better if it weren't so democratic. No, their job is to listen to those varied interests and to balance them.

The Framers of the Constitution understood that. But they could not guess the fantastic degree of organization and the huge amounts of money that would go into promoting such interests. In the late nineteenth century—the "Gilded Age," as Mark Twain called it—business grew bigger and bigger and the money power merged with the industrial power. The two became more unified, and monopoly, the domination of a whole industry, took hold. The struggle for control of the railroads typified the era. The rails ran across everything—industry, technology, agriculture, politics, morals. The empire builders made and used friends in high places—from a Speaker of the House of Representatives and future president, James A. Garfield, to future Vice President Schuyler Colfax. Senators, congressmen, and cabinet officials were welcomed into a holding company, the Crédit Mobilier, into which the profits from juicy construction contracts flowed for redistribution. The politicians, made stockholders for little or nothing, passed laws and appropriations bills benefiting what was now their own property. From the operations of the new tycoons many a political leader emerged a millionaire. The bribe had become the custom in political life. The vote of the legislator was for sale like any other product.

Senator Russell Long once said, "When you are talking in terms of large contributions . . . the distinction between a campaign contribution and a bribe is almost a hair's line difference." Of course legislators would like to believe that isn't so. A former staffer for two Democratic senators explained it to Richard Harris of the *New Yorker*:

One reason members of Congress insist that money doesn't influence them is that they . . . often become convinced of the rightness of their backers' causes without admitting it even to themselves. In time, they come to really believe that the guy who gives the big dough is the best guy and that helping him is in the public interest. . . .

Record amounts of money fueled the race for Senate seats in 1986. In California, the Democratic incumbent, Alan Cranston, raised $8 million, his Republican challenger, Ed Zschau, $8.5 million. In New York, the Republican incumbent, Alfonse D'Amato, got $6 million, his opponent, Democrat Mark Green, $1 million. In Florida, the two candidates raised $5 million each.

As the cost of campaigns soars, officeholders step onto a treadmill of fund-raising. And it threatens to move even faster. The journal *Campaigns and Elections* forecasts that the winners of the 1986 Senate races would need an average of $9 million to get reelected in 1992. Each senator has to raise an average of $125,000 a month every month during the six years in office to reach that goal.

A great influence on fund raising and therefore on politics is wielded by political action committees (PACs). These arose recently as citizens organized less around their political parties than around their own particular interests—farming, labor, corporations, oil, shipping, banking, poverty, civil rights, the environment, trucking, minorities. As they pushed for their own special programs, they set up PACs through which they contribute large sums to their favored candidates.

The 1986 elections saw the most expensive congressional campaigns in our history. The PACs contributed $132 million to the campaigns. The high financing brought mixed results at the polls. The Democrats gained six Senate seats, though they were outspent. In the House, they picked up a few more seats while outspending the Republicans in those contests. The Republicans collected five times as much as the Democrats: $179 million to $35 million. The results show there are some limits to what money can do. At least something depends on the quality of the candidates. Money doesn't guarantee winning, but it makes a big difference. It has a hidden effect, too. In some places, political analysts noted, potentially strong Democratic candidates were discouraged from running for the Senate because the Republicans started with so large a money advantage.

Political action committees hedged their bets by contributing to both parties in the 1986 Senate contests. That way their investment was a sure thing. By double giving, they knew they'd have access after the election to whichever candidate won. A study of PACs in nine Senate races showed that donations went to both parties nearly five hundred times.

It reminds us of what the cowboy actor and humorist Will Rogers said about the cost of election campaigns more than 50 years ago: "Politics has got so expensive it takes lots of money to even get beat with." The number of PACs has grown from a few hundred a decade ago to more than four thousand in 1987. The $132 million they pumped into congressional campaigns in 1986 was an all-time high. The House and Senate races together cost $450 million, up more than 30 percent in only three years. That sum was four and a half times the amount spent ten years ago.

How destructive the role of PACs can be was described by the *Dallas Times Herald*:

The power of PAC money threatens increasingly to turn members of Congress into legalized political prostitutes. It drives them to sell to the highest bidders their one most easily and legally saleable product—access. But worst of all, it erodes the public's confidence in the integrity of the congressional system.

The *Washington Post* adds that the present congressional campaign funding system "is fundamentally corrupt. Every citizen knows that. So does every legislator." And the *Des Moines Register* editorialized: "Enough! The money-changers have taken over the temples of democracy. They have bought the right to set the legislative agenda. They undermine public trust in the system."

Do something about it? People are still trying to curtail campaign spending of congressional candidates. There are limits on the amount of money individuals, PACs, and others may hand a candidate. But there's no limit on how much money a candidate can spend to get elected. Proposals for change have come from organizations such as Common Cause and the American Association for Retired People. The proposed laws offered would place spending limits by various means. Backers of reform are concerned that the escalating fund-raising forces legislators to give less time and attention to the issues. Not to mention the influence of all that money on decision making. Even if such bills go through, it's a question whether they won't be sidestepped as in the past. Those who have the most to gain by PAC gifts—members of Congress—are also the only ones who have the power to change the system. Can we expect members of Congress to act in the national interest when their election campaigns are funded more and more by pressure groups?

5

HI-TECH
CAMPAIGNING

Most would-be political managers prepared for their careers at law school or in political science courses, followed by on-the-job training. But professional politics has become such a big business in the last quarter century that you can now go to graduate school to earn a master's degree in how to run the show. Political management is what they call the complex and sophisticated new profession. Bright young men and women realize that it is now the professional political consultants who are the force that drives the system. They are the ones who make the candidate. To be experts, they must learn how to employ the latest technology to analyze, target, and reach every possible supporter for the candidate.

With the whole election process going high-tech, politics has become a "growth business," as one computer software executive puts it. These computer-wise entrepreneurs have found the new American brand of democracy to be a lucrative market as election costs multiply annually. By 1986 about 75 percent of the political campaigns across the country used computer technology. The process orchestrates almost every aspect of the campaign. The computer can pour out "personalized" letters focused on each voter's special concerns, plan media buys so that the candidate's TV commercials will reach the desired groups in the population, and on election day phone supporters with taped messages to get them out to the polls.

Let's say a government research bureau releases an important economic indicator for the month. The next day a candidate for Congress can call a computer in party headquarters in Washington and receive a sample press release advising how best to use those figures for his or her political advantage. Modern technology helps to gather such vital information and to transmit the message to the voting public. The technology replaces the old precinct captains who used to know the voting habits of every family in the neighborhood. Now the computer experts tap into all sorts of data banks and get far more political data than the old-style politicians could ever muster.

Reaching the voter at home with a highly personal message is one of the most effective uses for the computer. A candidate may want to send specialized letters to veterans, doctors, teachers, trade unionists, the aged, Jews, or Puerto Ricans. The highly selective message is sure to reach its highly selective audience, and sometimes in a form that appears to be handwritten but is really generated by the computer.

The computer can even single out groups of voters who

have been irregular or indifferent in their voting or party support and lure them to the polls on election Tuesday. Another computerized campaign tool was developed by the Republicans some years ago for their congressional candidates. In his or her office the candidate has a computer and a telephone modem, a device linking one computer to another over a telephone line. This sets up an information network centered in the Washington headquarters. The campaign manager in the field punches in various codes to find out all kinds of political information, from the opponent's voting record on whatever issue to the latest advice on organizing campaign volunteers. Even newer systems enable two offices to communicate without using a modem.

The administrative job of running the campaign office has also been eased by the computer. Software coordinates volunteers, lists potential contributors, keeps tabs on the candidate's schedule, and produces reports on campaign receipts and expenditures for the Federal Elections Commission. The computer firms busily design new software for political applications that change how things are done from year to year. This isn't only for presidential or congressional campaigns but moves downward into state and local contests.

The public think of themselves as voters and think of the computer as a machine. But to the computer, as the software companies see it, "the voter is a collection of numerous coefficients, calculated through a series of algorithms, revealing a pattern of daily behavior that reflects actions likely to be taken while inside a booth in the first week of November."

In the works is experimental software that not only spews out the data but suggests how to use it. This form of artificial intelligence wouldn't simply tell the candidate how far ahead the opponent is but would advise what to do to catch up.

The computers can even bring a personal phone call from the president into the voter's home. In the 1986 congressional campaign, President Reagan recorded a message filed at a mainframe in Chicago. At the right moment a switch was pulled, and the taped call shot out to 400 other computers throughout the country. The computers then placed hundreds of thousands of phone calls to registered Republicans on a single day. On each call people heard the president's voice urging them to vote. The next day, so the computer firm reports, an amazing number of people said, "The president called me on the phone last night." The same kind of service is now provided to local candidates.

Taking the pulse of the public is, of course, an essential function in campaigns. It's done most commonly through opinion polling run by political professionals. There are other polling groups that take their own polls periodically, often pursuing the same issues over years or months to see what shifts in public mood or point of view might have occurred. The media often combine in sponsoring polls during the campaigns. (Of course, the advertising agencies are the veteran users of polls to test market approval of their clients' products or to develop promotional campaigns to reach the consumers.)

The key ingredients in any poll include the size of the sample and its distribution—whether it reaches an ade-

quate proportion of blacks, working people, housewives, the middle class, or other groups. If a poll surveys a small number of people, it carries a greater margin of error. However, if the voter turnout is less than anticipated, the results may be quite different from what the polling predicted. There are wide variations in polling competence, and errors made can throw off results exceeding the sampling error of three to five percentage points that is generally factored in, depending on the sample size.

How reliable are political polls as indicators of public opinion? You may be sure that no one is likely to pay for a poll unless it satisfies his or her special interest. Pollsters usually don't ask questions purely in the public interest. Another consideration is that questions are often designed to give technical results; that is, the sponsors want usable answers. Some issues don't yield readily to a neat yes or no. The people queried may well have more to say than that but aren't given the chance to qualify or elaborate or refine their responses.

Campaign pollsters commonly survey voter opinion early in the race to determine their own candidate's particular strengths and weaknesses, as well as those of the opponent. Plans are then made to tailor the campaign to take advantage of what they've learned. Shifts in opinion are traced in follow-up polling, sometimes down to the last week or days. What's learned is put to use in the print and electronic media, especially in designing the TV spot commercials.

The image the candidate projects on the TV screen, given the expense and the brevity of that image, seems to be more important in winning votes than the candidate's genuine qualities. The makers of the TV spots work from the premise that it is the image, not the reality, that matters. One media consultant holds that elections are theater at heart. When he creates TV spots, he is "more interested in the dramatics than in the logical common sense of things."

How messages are delivered by the candidate has become as important as *what* is said. When style drives out content, politics becomes an empty game. The political media experts play to subliminal or subjective feelings, to perceptions of the world that may not have much to do with reality. They tailor messages to harmonize with those expectations. If a message conflicts with people's images, it may be disastrous for the candidate whose opponents don't deal with the facts. A classic case is Walter Mondale's TV appearances in the 1984 presidential election. He criticized some things he thought wrong with the United States that people weren't ready to listen to. Yet facing up to reality, to the true issues, is what meaningful politics should be about.

This trend in campaigning reminded the columnist Russell Baker of the days when things were different:

When I was a boy they had live politicians. Yes sir. Human flesh contained inside double-breasted suits. Not like nowadays when all you see is an empty suit on television and hear one of those oily voices trying to tell you there's a man inside there. . . . In those days, not only were these people inside politicians' suits, but if those people didn't have much weight inside the skull, they let you know it. Not everything about those old time pols was Jim Dandy, of course. For instance, when they wanted to deceive you about what they meant to do after getting elected, they would make a speech to you.

Honest to Betsy. Make a speech! Thirty, forty, fifty minutes of talk, talk, talk, all calculated to fool you about what you'd get if you made the mistake of voting for them.

In those days of course they didn't know that thirty seconds of television could fool more people than ninety minutes of oratory coming from an occupied suit. After they learned that, you quit seeing politicians in the flesh. . . .

Elections, like pro football games, are staged as media events. The important contests are between media consultants, not candidates. The press often pays as much attention to what the media consultants say as to what the candidates they work for say. The reporters know where the real story is. Politics is turned into a shadow campaign that fewer and fewer people care to watch. As the process goes on, the public becomes more sophisticated about the way TV is used to conceal a candidate's real character and attitudes. They know an image is being manufactured. They realize they are being treated by politicians not as intelligent voters but as an audience applauding teeth and haircuts. And they may wonder whether they are being fooled all the time or just some of the time as they observe presidential politics being turned into a branch of the entertainment industry. Even those candidates who are reluctant to, feel obliged to entertain or lose. The campaign is no longer about a policy for running the country but a competition for TV ratings.

Commercial advertising began to exert a major influence on political campaigns decades ago. It goes back to Dwight D. Eisenhower's presidential campaigns of the 1950s. The strategy and tactics applied then came from experts in the advertising agencies who took control of

the campaigns. Their advice has counted for much ever since. When President Reagan ran for reelection in 1984 he, too, relied heavily on their counsel. For that campaign, they blended softly lit small-town scenes, romantic landscapes, and strong patriotic images to echo the themes of highly successful automobile and soft drink campaigns of that year. Into that national mood of patriotism they keyed Ronald Reagan.

And it worked. To the ad agencies of Madison Avenue, it represented good casting. "There are some products you can sell with that technique, and there are some you can't," said a senior vice president of the J. Walter Thompson agency. "I think Ronald Reagan was the kind of product you can sell with the feel-good, glad-to-be-American approach."

But the media consultants don't let themselves get stuck in a groove. What works in one campaign may be wrong for another. Romance may give way to realism in concocting a candidate's image, but "realism" in quotes. Political commercials borrow freely from commercial advertisers. Use whatever will serve this season to grab the viewers' attention and make them believe *this* candidate is the *best*.

6

WHY SO FEW VOTERS AT THE POLLS?

How well does today's style of political campaigning work? It gets a candidate elected, perhaps. But if one measure of civic success is voter interest, then it works very badly. There has been a steady decline in voters going to the ballot box over the past twenty years. Back in 1960, 63 percent of the eligible voters cast presidential ballots. It dropped to 53 percent in 1984. In the 1986 congressional races, little more than a third of people eligible to vote did so. It was the lowest percentage since the war year of 1942.

Reagan's first victory, in 1980, was proclaimed a "landslide." But about half the voters stayed home; he won a majority of the half who came out to vote. That majority, however, amounted to less than 27 percent of the total number of eligible voters. You could hardly say the winner commanded the overwhelming support of the

American people. Yet the victory was interpreted that way by his party.

Analysts offer many explanations for the increasingly low turnout at the polls. They blame various barriers to voter participation. But several of these obstacles have been removed in the last few decades. The poll tax was outlawed as a voting requirement. Racial discrimination at the polling place has diminished. Residency, literacy, and linguistic requirements have been dropped in many places, and there are now bills before Congress to simplify the procedure by permitting mail-in and election-day registration. Young people between eighteen and twenty-one have been given the vote. These reforms, it was widely believed, would bring far more people to the polls on election day. Yet the trend is still downward.

Why? Because people are disillusioned with government, says Curtis B. Gans, director of the Committee for Study of the American Electorate. It's not just because of difficult voting requirements. Even if we succeed in enacting a simple federal registration law (the United States is the only Western democracy where the government takes no responsibility for registering its citizens to vote), studies suggest that it would boost voter turnout by no more than 9 percent.

Analysts of voting patterns say you get down to the real trouble when you recognize that the voting group whose turnout has declined the most since 1960 has been working-class and lower-class whites. The lower the family income, the fewer the number who vote. The result is an electorate increasingly middle and upper class. It is this section of the population whose vote the political parties compete for. In Europe, working-class people have long had labor or socialist parties to vote for. But here such voters are largely unorganized. The trade unionists now embrace less than one-fifth of the work force, and their influence in politics has shrunk considerably. The disaffection may reach into even wider sections. A 1987 poll revealed that about 50 percent of Americans believe the government is run by "a few big interests looking out for themselves."

One reason why the nonvoters feel the candidates have nothing to say to them is the heavy dependence on TV advertising, says the Committee for the Study of the American Electorate. Its glossy fakery, its negative messages, contribute to the drop in voting and to the negative public attitude toward the political process itself. Indifference—a big national yawn—has been building steadily despite tremendously important issues confronting the United States. The national trade and budget deficits, the huge sums expended on armaments, the sorry state of American manufacturing—all these demand the most intense thought and discussion that presidential aspirants and the public can give them.

Nevertheless, the real issues are often obscured or forgotten in the election campaign tactics of both major parties. The thirty-second TV snippets of images and catchphrases are commonplace now. Misleading as these snippets are, they cost vast sums to produce and place, and only richly endowed candidates can pay. It means that candidates with less funding, no matter how well qualified, can't afford to seek high office. It is another

example of how the money power shuts out a dissident point of view.

There are ways to reduce the influence of big money. Proposals have been made for Congress to adopt laws that would require free TV and radio time for all candidates. The Federal Communications Commission (FCC) could be empowered to issue regulations on the period for which such time shall be made available and for each level of office sought. Congress could set the principle, and the FCC could then hold public hearings before issuing such regulations. There would be nothing strange about this, for television and radio stations are, after all, licensed; the air waves belong to the public. It is surely in the public interest to reduce the high cost of elections and the harm the hidden influence of money does to democracy.

Reliance on TV political commercials can be connected to poor voter turnout in another way. As Ralph Nader, the consumer advocate, puts it, "What's getting lost, to the detriment of democracy, is the old-fashioned practice of going directly to the people—to whom, after all, candidates and officials are answerable." The voter can't talk back to a TV screen. When candidates do go out to meet the people, it doesn't assure us better results. But at least the two-way campaign could let citizens and journalists and the opponent, too, ask questions and demand honest answers.

Contrast this with what President Reagan actually did in the 1986 congressional elections when he tried to support the Republican candidates. He flew on Air Force One into twenty-two states, made fifty-four canned speeches (no candidates write their own speeches these days) that said so little of substance that not one of them was printed in full by any major newspaper. Reagan permitted no questions from the audience, none from reporters, and no news conferences for the White House press corps or the local press. Whatever he said went unchallenged. He left the impression he wanted without risk of a rebuttal.

His example has been followed by many other candidates for office. Why should they make themselves vulnerable when thirty-second TV and radio spots give them easy access to the voter and allow them to control their own media image?

Blame for failing to cast a ballot is often laid upon the voters themselves. They're accused of being ignorant, apathetic, stupid, prejudiced or of having no sense of civic pride. Beneath the censure of the voter is the assumption that the political system is just fine, the best we could have. If citizens don't want to vote, it means there's something wrong with *them.* All too rarely is nonparticipation seen as protest, as a justifiable reaction to an election that offers them nothing.

No wonder citizens complain that politicians promise one thing to get their vote and then do something else when they get into office. This doesn't mean that politicians are hypocrites or liars, though some of course are. Rather it's that politicians are trapped by what has happened to the system. To get elected, they need to win some amount of the popular vote and a large amount of the cash it takes to make the race. So to get into office and move on up, they often become servants of the rich and the mighty.

An often ignored fact is that voting is distressingly low not only in the regular elections, but even lower in the presidential primaries. These primaries may be decisive in the final choice of candidates. The winner of these primaries is chosen by only 16 percent of the United States's eligible voters. As for the other 84 percent of the country who live in the nonprimary and caucus states, they have no vote at all in this selection process.

When you get down to local elections, so few voters turn out that it often becomes hard to say the winner is a "popular" choice. Two-thirds stay away from the polls in municipal elections, unless the campaigns coincide with a state or national contest.

Again, low voter participation isn't the fault of the voters who sat at home. V.O. Key, the political scientist, made a study based on opinion surveys in six presidential elections. He found that voters did try to pick candidates who seemed to share their view of what the country needed. On the whole, he said, the electorate "behave about as rationally and responsibly as we should expect, given the clarity of the alternatives presented to it and the character of the information available to it." But those clear-cut alternatives and that factual information are precisely what's missing in too many political campaigns.

Whose fault is it that voters are uninformed? Don't blame it all on the political consultants, says one of them. William Zimmerman, head of a California firm, points the finger at the "two institutions in our society charged with the mission of informing the citizenry—the news media and the public schools. Students are rarely given the tools to understand how complex public policy op-

tions evolve behind the scenes in our halls of government." Furthermore, he adds, "a very small number of
newspapers and magazines allow serious coverage of public affairs." Thanks in part to the schools and the media,
he concludes, we've become a nation in which most voters
stay at home, in which 50 percent of those who read
newspapers do so only for the sports and entertainment
pages, and in which about a quarter of our adult population are too illiterate to read the news even if they
wanted to. Television news, he hastens to add, which
reaches more Americans than news through any other
media, demeans the news by giving so little and such
superficial attention to it.

What about the millions who *do* vote? Not all of them
vote because they find rational alternatives offered to them
in elections. In one survey, nearly 60 percent who took
part in the 1978 election said they didn't think the candidates they voted for believed their own statements. In
another study, over half of those who said they didn't
care at all about the election outcome voted anyway. In
the 1980 presidential contest, half the voters declared they
could find no difference between the candidates and between parties.

It's hard to know what to conclude from such facts.
Perhaps many people who have become cynical about the
political system vote just the same out of a sense of civic
responsibility. Many vote for the lesser of two evils. Both
candidates violate their interests, but they fear one would
be worse than the other. Then there are a great many
citizens—about a third of the electorate in recent times—
who call themselves "independent" because they find nei-

ther major party to their liking. Yet they go on voting, switching from one to the other of the party candidates when they find no real independent on the ballot.

Finally, there are people who vote simply because they feel that not to would be admitting how politically powerless they are. They have learned at school that this is a self-governing democracy and that voting is the essence of it—even when they don't see a genuine choice on the ballot.

7

REPUBLICANS, DEMOCRATS, AND WHO ELSE?

In the New England town meetings of early days the citizens could attend the sessions and vote directly on the policy proposals. Except for a handful of places where such direct democracy still operates, our system doesn't rest on individuals ruling themselves. Groups, not individuals, rule. If your vote is to count, it has to be part of group action.

That action operates through the two-party system. It developed in America but is by no means universal. While it is true of some English-speaking democracies, on the European continent a multiparty system prevails. China and the Soviet Union are one-party states, as are many other countries around the world. These totalitarian or authoritarian states maintain control at the cost of losing freedom and diversity. The multiparty countries give great room for diversity, but control is often lost through factionalism and party deadlock.

A word should be said here about the nature of party membership. Membership in either party is gained simply by indicating which one you wish to affiliate with when you register to vote. (You can indicate neither, which makes you an independent voter.) You don't take out any membership card or pay any dues, nor do you have to meet any qualifications for membership. There's a big difference between the party organization and the rank-and-file voters for that party. The leaders of the party are professional politicians who control its affairs, whether on the local, state, or national level. It's this inner core that is really "the party."

Clearly the Democrats in the past could command more popular support than the Republicans. It kept the Republicans a minority party for a long time. But in four out of the last five presidential elections—up to 1988— the Republicans showed they could combine, nationwide, the votes of the well-to-do with solid blocs of middle-class and working-class whites.

The old coalition of Franklin Roosevelt's years, made up of voters who knew or remembered the suffering during the Great Depression of the 1930s, lost much ground to an alliance of voters led by the nation's economic elite. American politics became polarized by income and race. By and large the people whose income is above the national median make up the Republicans. Those whose income is below it make up the Democrats. Up into the mid-1970s northern white Protestants of the upper class dominated the Republican party. Now they are only a third of the party because white southerners (traditionally Democrats) have swarmed into it. The party is now almost entirely white.

The Democrats meanwhile have gained from blacks the number they lost by the desertion of white southerners. The Voting Rights Act of 1965 enfranchised millions of blacks, mostly poor. As a result of intensive voter registration campaigns conducted by black leaders and black churches, some 8 million blacks now vote Democratic. Meanwhile white, evangelical, and born-again Christians converted en masse to the Republican party. When the great majority of fundamentalists shifted over, it strengthened the Republican ranks by some 8 million white voters.

Earlier, when Republicans controlled the White House during the Eisenhower, Nixon, and Ford years, they could not turn sharply toward a conservative economic and social policy. The reason? Too many voters still supported the Democratic principle that government should take care of those in need and out of work. But by the late 1970s that liberal brake had slipped badly. The Republicans had built up great strength through a right-of-center coalition that tilted sharply toward the prosperous classes. Under the Reagan administration, the Republicans had enough power to promote fiscal and spending policies that chiefly benefited the rich.

Even when the Democrats won control of both houses of Congress in 1986, they were able to do little to steer government in a liberal direction. This was so not only because Reagan was there to veto proposed laws he disapproved of but because the Democrats feared the big body of Republican voters out in the country, ready to back the president. The presence of a strong conservative force in the national electorate, equal to the liberal force, limits political choices on both sides. Democrats, who once talked of ways to help the poor and the needy by redistributing income more fairly, fell silent. Discussion of national health insurance, a guaranteed annual income, sustained federal financing for low-cost housing, the creation of jobs for the unemployed on public works, all faded into the background.

The sharp economic division between the two parties has greatly influenced how they function. The campaign reforms adopted during the Watergate crisis of the early 1970s changed the ways elections are financed. Contributions of $100,000 or more were eliminated and replaced by three different sources of cash: big givers able to hand out from $500 to $10,000; a larger group of small donors willing to respond to direct mail appeals; and the political action committees (PACs).

It turned out inevitably that with its middle- and upper-class supporters, the Republicans could count on raking in huge sums from people who liked the Republican policy of lower taxes for the well-to-do and cuts in domestic spending for the poor. The Democrats, with their lower-income following, could raise little by direct mail except from well-to-do liberals in scattered centers and from the elderly who can afford contributions and hope to prevent Republican gnawing at the social security system and their social security checks.

The imbalance in funding meant that the Democrats had to rely more than the Republicans on contributions from the PACs. Those who would give to either party want something in return. The PACs are not charitable agencies. The foremost PACs funding the Democrats have been real-estate developers, who profit by urban spending programs; contractors tied to city and state governments under Democratic control; and a host of corporate and trade association lobbyists. The trade unions, too, are large contributors to the Democrats.

The money raised under the campaign reforms powered the explosive growth of the Republican organization. It helped turn it into a hi-tech political machine. By getting well over $100 million a year to play with, the Republicans are able to carry out the many kinds of services described earlier.

The rewards from the Republican point of view have been substantial. They can be measured by the distribution of income and government benefits during the Reagan years. The median income of those in the bottom 40 percent (mostly Democrats) fell, while the income of those in the top 10 percent (mostly Republicans) rose. To take just one of the many findings offered by the Congressional Budget Office: the net effect of spending and tax cuts resulted in a loss of $1,100 between 1983 and 1985 for those making less than $10,000 a year. But those making more than $80,000 a year gained $24,260 as a result of government policy.

How important to the average voter is the political party? Decades ago the American public stopped believing in the great importance of the parties. People looked to the candidate, not the party, for the solution of political problems. Parties are not rejected altogether; they are thought of as useful vehicles for certain functions, but not as institutions inspiring great devotion. The candidates with their management teams and media experts now dominate politics.

The turbulent times of the 1960s saw the beginning of the change. Late in that decade party rules were upset by a reform movement seeking to democratize the nominating process. The role of state party officers was reduced to open up the process. Party bosses and party hacks had less to say. The new system made the primary elections far more important. Presidential candidates could no longer avoid risk by staying out of the primaries. All candidates had to compete in the early primaries in order to make their names nationally known, to get a head start over their rivals, and to win financial backing. Now the process has become so crucial that the race for the presidency starts long before the presidential election year begins.

Toward the end of the 1980s, the two political parties found themselves in near equal balance. Neither the Republicans nor the Democrats were a majority party. Each had developed a following of about 45 percent of the people who voted. Technically, that made them both minority parties. Without the backing of a majority of the voters it's hard for a political party to govern when it holds office. The equal balance works to prevent either the Republicans or the Democrats from coming up with a clear policy for running the country.

Yet that is what presidents are supposed to do: to establish leadership and direction, not only for their party, but for the country.

8

PRESIDENTS:
THEY COME
IN ALL KINDS

Let's go back for a moment to the Founding Fathers to locate the role of the presidency. When writing the Constitution, they divided government into three parts. The legislative branch would determine policy through the laws it enacted. The executive branch, headed by the president, would execute that policy. The judicial branch would settle disputes arising out of policy and its execution.

The creation of a presidency was something new. No other nation had such an office; under the Articles of Confederation there had been no chief executive. The delegates to the Constitutional Convention of 1787 were of two minds about a presidency. The struggling young nation made up of thirteen factions needed a national leader. The delegates didn't want only a figurehead, but how powerful should the national leader be? Some delegates were so nervous about kinglike rule that they proposed executive power should be placed in a group. Others wanted the president to share power with an elected council. In the end they decided to have one president and gave him considerable power. He would not only execute the laws of Congress but also command the armed forces. He would have charge of relations with foreign governments. He would appoint judges and many other major officials. He could veto laws passed by Congress.

Everyone agreed that the president should be a man of great character and proven ability. And everyone knew George Washington was the only choice for the first man to hold the highest office. He was elected unanimously. The country could not have chosen a more conscientious man. Carefully Washington took the reins of power, knowing he would be setting precedents with his every action. He believed he should use his powers to the full to carry out his responsibility. But he also knew that while Americans had full confidence in him, they feared the misuse of power by the unknown presidents to come.

With presidential powers defined only in general terms, the men who've held the office have used—or abused—its authority to carry out what they consider their mandate to be. Presidents have been strong, weak, energetic, lazy, brilliant, stupid, bold, timid, honest, corrupt, narrow-minded, generous, humane, bigoted. Whatever their personal traits, the general tendency has been to expand presidential power. Partly this was the inevitable effect of the country's enormous growth in size and complexity and partly the effect of the political beliefs of the man holding office.

The president is the only national officer elected by the citizens of the whole country. It is easy for him to assume that all the power in the land is in his hands. It is easy for a president to think that it is *his* will that counts, and only his will. Presidents who believe that can act like emperors. They command; the people obey. One president who acted this way—Richard Nixon—was forced to resign under threat of impeachment.

On the other hand, a president may see himself as one political leader among many. He knows his authority is based on wider support, but the other politicians he must deal with each have their own power base. Such a president has ideas about what the country needs, and he does his best to persuade the Congress to do what he thinks best. But he does not order the legislators around, nor does he stray beyond his constitutional authority and violate the law to get what he wants.

You wonder how any president can stand the awesome responsibility. He has so many hats to wear. He is leader of his party, he is chief executive, he designs foreign policy, he manages the economy, he is chief legislator in that he proposes programs for the Congress to enact, he commands the armed forces, he speaks for the American people. Each job requires the handling of power with skill and wisdom. In any one day in the Oval Office he may have to switch hats a dozen times to meet what the situation demands.

The man at the levers of control has enormous power. Abraham Lincoln believed it was boundless: "See if you can fix *any* limit," he said. But there *are* limits, however broadly defined. The Constitution requires every president to take this oath: "I do solemnly swear (or affirm) that I will faithfully execute the Office of the President of the United States, and will to the best of my Ability, preserve, protect and defend the Constitution of the United States."

From World War II on, however, some political scientists hold that presidents have taken on more and more power to the point where it is "flatly inconsistent with both the intentions of the Founders and the requirements of a democratic political order." On the other hand, some scholars argue that presidential power is not what it seems to be. They observe that a president may want to do certain things, but if he cannot persuade the others in the political arena, he cannot command. When President Harry S. Truman was leaving office, he pointed to his seat in the Oval Office and said of his successor, General Dwight D. Eisenhower, "He'll sit here. And he'll say, 'Do this! Do that!' And *nothing* will happen. Poor Ike . . . it won't be a bit like the Army. He'll find it very frustrating."

A president has to make deals, negotiate, compromise, and will succeed only to the extent of his influence. Of course, his authority and status give him greater influence than others have. He can threaten a veto, promise appointments, use his unlimited access to the media, manipulate budgets to coerce or cajole others into support. Everyone in Washington knows that their own jobs are linked in one way or another to presidential decisions. They need his goodwill, and they fear his enmity.

They have reason to. President Nixon had strong ideas about the use of power in dealing with people he wanted to get something from. "One day," he said, "we'll get them—we'll get them down on the ground where we want them. And we'll stick our heels in, step on them hard and twist—right?" Then he turned to his secretary of state, Henry Kissinger, and added, "Henry knows what I mean— just like you do it in the negotiations, Henry—get them on the floor and step on them, crush them, show them no mercy."

It is the president who decides what to project as the major issues on which Congress should act. Whether they like or dislike him, members of Congress cannot duck an issue he insists upon. Even when citizens elect to Congress a majority that opposes the president, he still has the power to write the agenda the Congress must consider. Of course, they may or may not defeat his program.

Presidents have serious differences with the Congress from the very nature of their respective offices. The president is supposed to consider the good of the whole nation; a member of Congress, the good of his or her district or region. This means president and Congress are pushed and pulled by conflicting interests. Then, too, the president has to think about the probable effect of a policy on the party as a whole. Members of Congress take a position on the basis of how it will affect their political career in their own district. Sometimes members of Congress are pressured so hard by a special interest group in their district that they will depart from what their party is said to stand for to please that bloc of voters back home.

When a president is weak or indecisive, he may fail to give the country any direction. Without his leadership, drift and inaction follow. Again, a president may put forth an unwise or poorly thought out proposal, which may harm not only his own standing but damage his party. The Congress is mindful of that hazard to its own political fortunes and may quickly put the blame on the White House. Often even the congressional members of his own party grow irritated with the president. They criticize him; he rebukes them. They may feel left out on the many occasions when a president formulates his program without any consultation with the party leaders in Congress. If congressional members of the president's party have no voice in policy, they may refuse to follow the president's lead.

In the way our system is set up, the president does not govern alone. American government is a system of multiple power centers. But its effective functioning depends upon presidential leadership. Things happen only if someone takes charge. When that someone—the president— takes charge, it isn't always for the best. He may use his office to do great good or great harm. In the 1970s, President Nixon was driven from office because he perceived himself as an absolute authority who could order people to commit illegal acts and then conspire to cover up those acts. He approved a plan for burglaries and other acts against opponents of the Vietnam War. The break-in at Watergate was only the last of his misdeeds, the one which brought ruin upon him. To escape impeachment he became the first president to resign from office.

Scarcely a dozen years later, in the mid-1980s, another president, Ronald Reagan, was criticized for similar abuse of power. Like Nixon, he believed that the president is above the law. In 1977, three years after his downfall,

Nixon was interviewed for TV by David Frost. Frost asked Nixon whether the law does not bind a president when he acts in what he believes is in the interest of national security. Here is the dialogue:

NIXON: When the President does it, it means that it is not illegal.
FROST: By definition.
NIXON: Exactly. Exactly. If the President, for example, approves something because of the national security . . . then the President's decision in that instance is one that enables those who carry it out, to carry it out without violating a law.

In President Reagan's case, his actions in permitting the sale of arms to Iran, when it was against government policy, and then letting the profits from those arms sales be channeled to the military aid of the Contras fighting against the government of Nicaragua, led to a congressional investigation that culminated in an official report late in 1987. The national newspaper *USA Today* commented on the findings of that report:

A small, powerful group, dubbed the "cabal of the zealots" by the committee's majority, was able to usurp powers reserved for the elected representatives of the people. Among the cabal were the President's national security adviser, the director of Central Intelligence, and an aggressive Marine colonel assigned to the White House.
None of them trusted democracy. They ignored laws. They kept the President in the dark. They lied to Congress, treating it not as the voice of the people but as a nuisance to be overcome. The Constitution they simply forgot.
When the cabal was exposed, some of its members destroyed evidence, boasted of their noble intentions, and suggested to Congress that they were accountable to their own particular view of right and wrong, not to the law.

That is intolerable. . . .

The committee majority correctly placed the blame for failing to control the cabal in the Oval Office. . . .

It said the President failed to monitor his subordinates, allowing them to believe any action to free the hostages or aid the Nicaraguan Contras was acceptable. . . .

While the President has acknowledged his accountability, he has yet to condemn the actions of the cabal.

He should . . . make clear that the law takes precedence over politics, and to help assure that this type of activity can never be repeated. . . .

When presidents in the face of crisis defy the Constitution and the law, it does terrible damage to the bonds of trust that link the people and their leaders in a democracy. After the Iran-Contra affair, one Republican strategist said, "People in this country are ready to think the worst of almost anyone." The makers of the Constitution were not at fault. They did not believe in the perfect wisdom of any leader. They saw America's future as best served by a system of overlapping powers. They hoped that checks and balances would restrain the arrogant— whether in the executive or legislative branch—and oblige our elected representatives to debate the issues publicly and to examine critical questions in the light of national purpose.

The Watergate and Iran-Contra scandals remind us that there really are no institutional or legislative protections against a president who secretly abuses the people's trust. If a president looks hard enough, he can find loopholes in the laws or create devices to get around the laws, no matter how many times we try to improve procedures. Perhaps the only safeguard is to take sufficient care to choose a president who will faithfully execute the laws we already have.

That is never easy to do. In previous chapters, we've seen how the modern election system makes selection of the right candidate so difficult. Yet what happens after a president is elected and takes office? George E. Reedy, former special assistant to President Lyndon B. Johnson, has written much about the isolation, the air of unreality, and the nearly unchecked power that can corrupt anyone who sits in the Oval Office. From long personal observation, he says that in the atmosphere of the White House idealism and devotion do not flourish. Instead, the White House provides "an ideal cloak for intrigue, pomposity and ambition." The biggest problem a president faces, Reedy goes on to say, is "that of maintaining contact with reality."

Built into the presidency is a series of devices that tend to remove the president "from all of the forces which require most men to rub up against the hard facts of life on a daily basis." Because the man at the top is supposed to grapple with vastly important problems, he is kept free of all petty annoyances, and treated "with all of the reverence due a monarch," says Reedy. No one speaks to him unless spoken to first. No one ever tells him to come off it when he makes silly or unreasonable demands. Every little need, whim, or desire is taken care of by a host of servitors.

The privileges given him as soon as he enters the White House may startle the president for a time—but only briefly. He soon comes to believe this is all his just due and not because of the office but because he himself is deserving of all this deference. In his own eyes he becomes untouchable, unapproachable except upon his gracious permission. He is not to be called to account by any other person or body. Even the news media treat a new president with awe—at least for a time.

It is this heady feeling, Reedy firmly believes, that helps account for such disasters as met Johnson, Nixon, Reagan, and others before them:

The environment of deference, approaching sycophancy, helps to foster another insidious factor. It is a belief that the president and a few of his most trusted advisers are possessed of a special knowledge which must be closely held within a small group lest the plans and the designs of the United States be anticipated and frustrated by enemies. It is a knowledge which is thought to be endangered in geometrical proportion to the number of other men to whom it is passed. Therefore, the most vital national projects can be worked out only within a select coterie, or there will be a "leak" which will disadvantage the country's security.

When the president and his small band of advisers make their secret decisions, the matter is not put to public debate. They do not defend their positions before the Congress or the people. Even the most brilliant and best informed of us, when forced to answer critical questions, discover we don't have all the answers. A public airing of many a presidential decision—in advance of the action that follows—might prevent many of the disasters the country is put through. But in the White House the fawning upon the president, and the tightly held reins, frustrate this need.

Reedy knocks in the head the popular belief that the

office of the presidency ennobles the man in the White House, stretching him so that he can meet any issue. Reedy contends that the office neither elevates nor degrades a president. He is what he was when he took power in his hands. The office magnifies whatever those qualities are, only now everyone can see them operate on the national or international stage. The public that may scarcely have noticed him before, now sees him through the media telescope. It is his own character and personality that will govern his conduct in office.

Every president shoulders a heavy burden of making political decisions upon which life or death may depend for hundreds of millions the world round. Yet his daily tasks are not overwhelming. A huge army of subordinates in every department of government is delegated to do the everyday chores. No president dies of overwork in that respect. The burden is one of responsibility for improving or spoiling the lives of Americans, for helping or harming them, for saving or destroying their lives.

In the end, what the president must do comes down to two things: He has to decide those policy questions that can't be handled by a computer, by quantitative calculations. He also has to convince the people that his decisions are the right ones, so that he can carry them out without tearing apart the fabric of society.

9

WHAT CONGRESS DOES OR FAILS TO DO

In the making of the Constitution, compromise played the problem-solving role it has performed in American politics ever since. We saw in Chapter 3 how the Constitutional Convention settled the issue of power between the larger and smaller states.

With each state, regardless of the size of its population, allotted two seats in the Senate, the smaller states may swing more weight in the voting than the larger. A senator from Vermont, where 500,000 people live, can have thirty-four times the influence that a senator from New York, with its 17,000,000 people, has. In practice, the equal representation of the states in the Senate operates to overrepresent the mainly rural states and to underrepresent the mainly urban states.

The House has the sole power to initiate all bills for raising revenue. Only the Senate can approve treaties and certain appointments. Other powers granted Congress include enacting taxes, providing for defense, declaring war, fixing tariffs, coining money, and establishing post offices. Congress is given the power to pass all laws "necessary and proper" to carry out its specific assigned functions. (The full text of what the Constitution says about the powers of Congress is in Article I, Section 8.)

But what the Constitution says and what the Congress actually does may be two different things. Take the power "to declare war." This power is granted to Congress and to no one else. Yet presidents have sent our armed forces beyond our borders over 165 times in our rather short history. (We have taken part in seven officially declared wars.) Neither the Korean nor the Vietnam wars were declared. Trying to take back its authority, the Congress passed a War Powers Act in 1973 (over a presidential veto). It declares that the president must inform the House and Senate within forty-eight hours of placing American troops where they might be involved in fighting. The president has to bring the troops home within ninety days unless both houses vote to let them stay. Nevertheless, presidents still find ways to dodge the provisions of the War Powers Act.

In considering what Congress does, or fails to do, bear in mind the two obligations it has. First, Congress is responsible for writing and overseeing laws to benefit the nation as a whole. Second, it represents particular constituencies and interest groups in the states and districts that vote it into office. Textbooks usually stress what the formal powers of Congress are. But what about how Congress actually works? Does it produce what was intended? Do the results give us a sense of an intelligent national policy on the basic social and economic issues that affect all citizens?

The congressional process may work smoothly as negotiation and compromise take place. But efficiency can't be the sole measure to apply. Who benefits by the legislative results? What interest groups are satisfied and which are not? Are the interests of sizable sections of the population totally ignored?

Some time ago a political scientist made a detailed study of the lawmaking process as it produced a specific piece of legislation—the Full Employment Act of 1946. Professor Stephen Bailey found the process to be "almost unbelievably complex." Describing how policy is worked out, he said the flow of things

appears to be the result of a confluence of factors streaming from an almost endless number of tributaries: national experience, the contributions of social theorists, the clash of powerful economic interests, the quality of Presidential leadership, other institutional and personal ambitions and administrative arrangements in the Executive Branch, the initiative, effort and ambitions of individual legislators and their governmental and nongovernmental staffs, the policy commitments of political parties, and the predominant culture symbols in the minds of both leaders and followers in the Congress.

Pulling and tugging at this tangled web are the conflicting desires of most Americans. They ask two things of Congress: laws that advance the general welfare, and laws that satisfy their own personal interests. So when the public looks at the results of congressional action, it sees it "cross-eyed." People measure what is going on

both by the standard of the national good and by the opposing standard of selfish concern.

A Nobel Prize winner in economics holds that the balance tips toward self-interest. Professor James M. Buchanan won the prize in 1986 for developing new methods of analyzing how economic and political decisions are made. He holds that in both worlds—politics and economics—people seek to secure their own interests, rather than those of society. He fears that moral constraints, vital to a healthy and effective society, are breaking down. The relentless chase after selfish interest, whether individual or national, creates misery for all.

Professor Buchanan's work focused on the forces determining how government decides what to spend money on. He looks at politicians and voters and asks, What does it *pay* them, or what does it *cost* them, to make changes in public expenditures? He concludes that like the rest of society, politicians are motivated by self-interest. They tend to ignore the general welfare and take actions more likely to secure election or gain additional power.

But other political thinkers are not as negative or cynical. They believe legislators are also influenced by what they truly believe is in the public interest. Moreover, in American history, there is evidence of legislators who held firmly to their own convictions even at the risk of increasing the likelihood of defeat at the polls. If a legislator's constituents are concerned only with their own narrow self-interest, and the legislator himself or herself seeks only to serve such selfishness, then there is no broad-based public interest to appeal to in trying to improve social policy. Isn't there such a thing as *enlightened* self-interest?

Putting aside the moral question, a look at the way Congress is set up and operates indicates how hard it is to get things done. Power in Congress rests chiefly in permanent committees in each chamber. (The House in 1986 had thirty-one standing committees and the Senate had twenty-four.) The committees decide the destiny of bills. They rewrite some, approve some, and bury most. Each committee has various subcommittees. Those who chair the committees and subcommittees get to their important posts mostly by seniority. In both the House and Senate, the party with a majority controls the selection of chairpersons of that chamber.

The leadership of the House is elected by the majority party. Number one is Speaker of the House, who serves as leader of the majority party and of the entire body itself. The Speaker has great power in determining legislative priorities. The number two job is the House majority leader. He or she acts as the partisan spokesperson, pushing for his or her own party's program. The number three person is the majority whip; he or she keeps track of votes on the floor and serves as liaison between the leadership and his or her party's members.

The Speaker is expected to use all the tools at his or her disposal to get legislation enacted. In recent years, however, that task has become much harder. For the Congress began to change dramatically in the 1970s. Its membership is now younger, better educated, and more independent than before. The members do not submit easily to the regimentation the House Speaker could once count on. The Speaker can no longer appeal to party loyalty and discipline to get things done. Personal rather than party relationships seem to count for more. Now the Speaker has to persuade, rather than order, people to do what he wants.

Historically, the president has usually been the one to set a legislative agenda before Congress, with the Speaker reacting to it. But a Speaker who is more assertive will not simply react passively to the president's proposals; he or she takes the initiative. The Rules Committee, controlled by the Speaker's party, dictates what legislation can be brought on to the floor. The Steering and Policy Committee of the majority party names all chairpersons of the committees and subcommittees. (There are over 350 now in the House and Senate, each with a fixed legislative area.)

Each of these committees is a sort of petty kingdom. Easy access to television gives the members a certain prominence even if they do little inside the Congress. It leads to more independence from the House leadership and diffuses the power. Often the committee chairpersons pursue their own agendas in the field of their operations. Their committees write the bills and then seek support from the leadership and the rest of the House.

For newly elected members of Congress the search for appointment to the right committee is desperately important. Which committee will best serve your constituents' needs and your own personal ambition? The members bargain in back rooms with congressional bigwigs and lobby up front for votes from their colleagues. While new members seek their first assignment, the veterans may maneuver to shift from one committee to another with greater prestige or to another better suited to their constituents' interests. Naturally the veterans get the best assignments, leaving few seats for the freshmen on the more popular committees. The prime choices are those dealing with taxes, appropriations, and the budget. (Money, money, money.) Another House committee hotly pursued is Energy and Commerce. Why? Because it's a good fundraising opportunity. Its members tend to get fatter contributions from the political action committees concerned with these questions.

Assignment is also partly luck—what impression the newcomer makes. Is he or she "a nice guy"? Or "a pain"? Each member hopes to chair some subcommittee because of the extra staff that comes with the job. The committee chair, always of the majority party, chooses the staff for his or her side, while the ranking minority member picks the people for his or her side. The majority and minority committee heads have an important impact on the functioning of the committee panel and on the quality of its output. When a committee's bill goes to the floor, the staff provide support in the management of the debate for the party they work for.

Standing behind every single member of Congress is a staff. (The House has about 11,000 aides and the Senate 7,000.) These aides often exercise a heady amount of power. While the member makes all the final decisions on voting or, if a chairperson, on what issues to press in his or her committee and how to write the bills, the aides are the people who do the research, conduct the negotiations with business and industry or whomever else is concerned, determine the dimensions of the bill, and gain support for it. Aides are drawn from many sources. Some are veterans of government departments or agencies. Others are bright young lawyers, economists, or sociologists hired for their expertise. The senators and representatives rely heavily on the input of aides in dealing with other members of the Congress and their aides, with the lobbyists, with the media, and with every element of society whose support is needed to accomplish some goal.

Within Congress there are numerous caucuses, that is, groups of members bound by some common interest. A caucus may form around a specific issue (the Steel Caucus) or a region (the Sunbelt Caucus) or party affiliation (the Democratic Study Group). The Rural Caucus, the Hispanic Caucus, the Human Rights Caucus, the Women's Caucus, the Black Caucus, and even the Mushroom Caucus are among some forty caucuses officially registered as Legislative Service Organizations. The caucus offers a way for legislators to form influential alliances and to gain ready access to all-important information.

Some of these groups have no offices, charge no dues, and jump into action only as hot issues come up. Others operate with full-time staff, requiring membership dues that range from a few hundred to several thousand dollars a year. Members of Congress will rely on a caucus for help when they don't have the staff to follow through on the issue themselves or need a research report. Caucuses may issue newsletters, produce regular briefing papers, and supply specially requested research reports. Caucus strength rises when congressional budgets are ample and falls when expenses have to be cut.

Although the power of Congress is derived from the Constitution and the law, the *use* of it depends in part on the general situation in the country. In times of crisis—war, a great depression—the executive branch takes more power unto itself. When President Truman ordered United States forces into Korea and when Presidents Johnson and Nixon sent troops into Vietnam, without any declaration of war by Congress, Congress became little more than a cheerleader or rubber stamp for the White House.

But when things are rather calm, the legislative branch exerts more authority. If public opinion is very strong on a particular issue and voices itself through massive action, then Congress can put through measures over a president's opposition, even when that president is popular. The issue of the environment is an example. In both the 1970s and then the early 1980s Nixon and Reagan paid little attention to environmental protection. Yet the rising popularity of that issue became so great that neither president could prevail against public pressure to do something about it. Many protective laws were passed, and despite vetoes by both Nixon and Reagan, Congress overrode their vetoes overwhelmingly.

How does a bill move through Congress? To map its complex progress as simply as possible:

- A. A bill is introduced into the House of Representatives or into the Senate.
- B. It's taken up by a committee, or more often
- C. distributed to various subcommittees for extensive hearings, or
- D. reported *out* of subcommittee *to* full committee, where it may be watered down, expanded, or fully rewritten. It then goes to

E. the Rules Committee, which may make further changes or replace it entirely with another preferred bill. Then

F. it reaches the floor of the House (or the Senate) where it may be further amended during debate, referred back to committee for more study, or passed.

G. If passed, it must go through much the same process in the Senate (or the House), should the Senate (or the House) decide to take it up.

H. When the Senate and House each pass a somewhat similar bill but fail to pass the same version of the bill, the differences have to be bargained out in conference committees made up of several senior members of each house. The rewritten bill then goes back to both houses.

I. Both houses vote on the rewritten bill.

J. If a bill fails to make it through both houses before the next congressional election, and its backers persist, it must be reintroduced in the next Congress and the whole process started again.

K. If a bill gets through this labyrinth and is not vetoed by the president, it becomes the law. But it may only be an authorization act. That simply brings a program into existence—on paper. Congress has to vote funds to finance the official policy. The entire legislative process has to be repeated for the appropriations bill. Sometimes no appropriations are voted to bring the program alive.

To an outsider, it seems amazing that anything gets legislated. Bills have so many hurdles to jump that most are easily crippled or killed. Some historians assert the process was designed to slow down action. The Founding Fathers, most of them upper class, wanted to put up barriers against mass sentiment for sweeping changes in the laws. The two separate houses of Congress and the swarm of committees and subcommittees make it easier to ignore bills, gut them, or bury them.

For the record: in the 99th Congress (1984–1986), 7,522 measures were introduced in the House and 4,080 in the Senate. A total of 664 bills were enacted.

In looking at the way Congress votes, a few points are worth keeping in mind. George Reedy's study of how the Senate operates makes useful observations. Voting in that chamber, he notes, usually comes up after a long period of negotiation. History shows that on major issues, the Senate divides into three blocs: those strongly opposed, those strongly in favor, and between them a large middle group—the decisive bloc. The two extremes negotiate with the center in the hope of winning enough of it over to make a majority on a compromise bill. The makeup of the three blocs of course shifts constantly as the issues change.

Rarely does a legislative proposal command a majority on its own. It becomes law only by delicate dickering. The public calls the process "wheeling and dealing" or "horse-trading" and considers it a bad thing. However, this process is the essence of politics; it takes people with this kind of talent to make democracy work. They are sensitive to the time when a coalition is ripe enough for a bill to go through. A bill will not be passed in the Senate unless at least fifty-one senators are won over (or sixty-seven if there should be a veto).

When members of Congress cast votes, it isn't done in isolation from everything else. Members of Congress are aware that how they vote on any given question becomes part of their long-term record. Their votes will be weighed by friend and foe when the next election rolls round. Each vote cast is like another daub on their self-portrait, and it sets up expectations for their next vote, too. Votes are often made to pay off political debts owed to others in or out of Congress. Votes are also made to place others under an obligation to pay off the congressional vote cast in the future. So a vote isn't just a thing in itself: it's cast in a marketplace where bargains are constantly being struck.

Some analysts of congressional operations point out that bills to benefit business tend to move through this process smoothly. But bills intended to help the poor, the deprived, the weak, the unorganized, may often be ignored or handled with painfully slow deliberation.

Speedy action can occur: bills for armaments are an example. High-cost weapons bring jobs into congressional districts and states. Components of the B-1 bomber, for instance, have been made in more than forty states. The gigantic military buildup during the Reagan administration met little resistance in Congress until nearly the end of Reagan's last term. (Naturally, when a president's ratings in the polls slip, Congress rediscovers its independence.)

On the other hand, measures to provide affordable day care for children whose mothers are obliged to work had a hard time getting attention in Congress for several years. Families below the poverty level have little political clout. It took dramatic headlines about the tragic deaths of several youngsters because their mothers were working and couldn't afford decent child care to rouse public feeling.

That galvanized Congress into action. Late in 1987 a broad coalition of lawmakers introduced a $2.5 billion measure to help states improve the quality and expand the availability of day-care service for the 9 million children of preschool age whose parents work.

Clearly, big business has great power to shape legislation. But the legislators themselves don't find it hard to identify with the rich. A great many members of Congress live on far better incomes than most Americans. More than a third of the U.S. Senate is made up of millionaires. Nearly everyone in Congress has an income of about $100,000 a year. Their federal salaries ($77,400 in both houses) and their income from investments and other sources place them in the top 1 percent bracket. It does not mean they cannot feel with the needy. Many do. But their way of living is a long way from the lives of Americans their votes influence deeply. Republican Representative Mickey Edwards from Oklahoma once said, "Every time we vote, we change people's lives, we increase or destroy their opportunities, we provide them with incentives or we diminish their hopes for the future."

Still, people who don't travel in jammed subways or buses at rush hour make transportation policy. People who don't pick lettuce or shoulder the debts of a small family farm make agricultural laws. People who don't work in a sawmill or a coal mine make safety rules. People who never sweated out a line in a charity clinic decide on medical insurance. People who were never hungry or homeless vote on welfare programs. Yes, most representatives in Congress lead unrepresentative lives.

Some in Congress, while blind to the needs of their

fellow citizens, have their eyes wide open when it comes
to spotting ways to steal from the public treasury. From
World War II to 1980 more than sixty members of Congress or their aides were indicted or convicted of bribery,
influence peddling, extortion, and other crimes. Several
representatives and one senator were convicted in the
early 1980s for taking bribes from FBI agents posing as
Arab businessmen.

When its members get into such trouble, the Congress
is slow to investigate and punish its colleagues. Both the
Senate and the House have ethics committees, which rarely
investigate charges made against members. When the Senate did look into a charge that several senators had profited from a fat slush fund run by oil companies, it dropped
the inquiry quickly without calling corporate witnesses
ready to name names. No one went to jail.

There are so many ways—in government as well as in
business—to take personal and often illegal advantage of
one's position to enrich oneself at the expense of the
public. Perhaps more important is the way members of
Congress help special interests to enrich themselves by
the "logrolling" method. That's the means by which one
congressional faction deals with another to benefit special
interest groups. Factions will combine strengths to gain
majority support for a piece of selfish legislation. (This is
different from political compromise to achieve something
for the *public* benefit.) Let's say a faction backing leases
of public land to an oil company will trade votes with a
faction backing cash supports for big farmers. Their deal
operates *against* the interests of a public powerless to
apply pressure.

Let's look at the differences between the way senators and representatives operate, and the way they are perceived by the public. In the House, members serve only a two-year term, while in the Senate it is six years. The shorter period keeps representatives closer to their constituents. They are forced to be in touch, because the minute they take the oath of office they start running for reelection. They take full advantage of the wide range of benefits and privileges they have voted themselves. Trips home are free, and they get big allowances to run their offices and staffs. It helps them provide many services for the voters. A voter may say he dislikes the way that old Jones voted on this issue, but darn it, he came through when my son needed help from the Veterans Administration.

By acting as ombudsmen for their district in getting action from the huge federal bureaucracy, representatives win voter loyalty. It's easier to do that when you represent a congressional district that's quite small in contrast to the whole state a senator has to work for. A senator has to deal more often with conflicting interests, and his or her support for one interest may alienate another.

Citizens identify a senator more closely with national issues than with local ones. Senate campaigns are more likely to be fought on major questions. By taking sides, a senator will inevitably make enemies of people on the other side. However, because a senator serves for six years, he or she isn't so hard-pressed. There's time for voters to forget or forgive something a senator did they didn't like, and time for that senator to build more slowly and steadily his or her base for support.

An interesting development is the increasing frequency with which House members are reelected to office. In the 1986 election, 396 representatives sought a new term, and only 6 lost their seats. That's a reelection rate of nearly 99 percent, the highest in history. That is often partly because they come from a district where one party is so dominant the other has little or no chance to win. Ever since World War II, members of the House have been staying in Congress longer and making a career out of it. Yet not so far back, the Congress was seen as a brief chapter in a life that could take other turns. To serve in the House wasn't viewed as the crowning achievement of a career. In the Senate it was somewhat different. The Senate, a far more august body, boasted men like Daniel Webster, Henry Clay, and John C. Calhoun, who were acclaimed as great statesmen. (A note for the curious: about 11,700 people have served in Congress: roughly 10,000 in the House and 1,700 in the Senate.)

10

THE LAST WORD
ON THE LAW

If it is the Congress that makes the laws, and the president who sees they are carried out, it is the Supreme Court that resolves any disputes about the laws. Its judges can decide, in cases brought before it, when Congress goes beyond its proper authority and when acts of the president or his assistants are unlawful or unconstitutional.

While the Constitution provided for a system of United States courts, separate from the courts of each state, the Supreme Court was the only court it mentions specifically. How many judges the Court would have was left to Congress, as well as how many lower courts to set up. As it stands, there are nine Supreme Court justices and two kinds of federal courts—the district courts and the appellate, or appeals, courts.

To shield judges from pressure, under the Constitution they serve "during good behavior." Unless they commit a crime or become insane or too ill to function, they hold office for life. Thus they need not fear a majority's anger when they protect the rights of an unpopular minority.

In its first century, the Court played a big part in protecting private property from state interference and building a strong central government. Later, the Court tackled the difficult problems of race, civil liberties, and criminal justice. The Court shifts ground from time to time, overturning earlier decisions to strike out on new paths of interpretation. A classic example is the *Plessy v. Ferguson* decision of 1896, when the Court ruled that a state law requiring segregation was legal provided that facilities for blacks were as good as those for whites. This "separate but equal" decision encouraged segregation in railroad cars, hotels, restaurants, hospitals, sports, and schools. It was the law until 1954, when the Warren Court made one of the most important rulings in the Court's history. It decided in the case known as *Brown v. Board of Education of Topeka, Kansas,* that it was unconstitutional for states to maintain separate schooling for black and white children. It held that a separate education was by its very nature an unequal education. The unanimous decision said that segregation had harmful effects on all children, white as well as black.

In the early 1900s the Court began to pay attention to economic and social data as underpinning to legal arguments. The pioneer case was *Muller v. Oregon* (1908) when a lawyer, Louis D. Brandeis (later a Supreme Court justice), gathered research to show that long hours of work injured the health of women and therefore the health of children they might have. This threatens the well-being of the public at large, he held. The Court then ruled that the state of Oregon had the right to limit the working hours of women laundry workers.

Legal experts and historians have long argued over what justifies the Court's extraordinary power. The Constitution doesn't say specifically that the Court can declare federal laws unconstitutional. The first time the Court chose to do that was in the *Marbury v. Madison* decision (1803). It was a minor question that arose over the appointment of a justice of the peace in the District of Columbia. But when Chief Justice John Marshall held that a clause in the law creating certain federal courts was unconstitutional, he set the great principle of judicial review. Fifty-four years went by before the Court again used that power to decide if a law violated the Constitution, in the explosive *Dred Scott v. Sandford* decision of 1857. It declared blacks had no rights that the whites were bound to respect and that blacks could not rightfully become citizens of the United States. In effect, the Court declared the Missouri Compromise and all other anti-slavery laws unconstitutional.

There are those who think the Court should merely interpret the Constitution's text, figuring out what the Constitution meant to those who wrote it, when they wrote it, and do nothing more. Supporters of this original intent viewpoint believe that the Court should defer to the other branches of government as much as possible. But if it always did that, critics of this view say, we would never have had *Brown v. Board of Education* as well as

other major decisions, and the Court's ability to protect minority rights would be ended.

On the other hand, if the Supreme Court is free to go beyond so-called original intent, where does it draw the line? By relying on the accumulated wisdom of the past stored in legal tradition? Wouldn't that reliance on the long line of the past prevent innovation and arrest the creative development of law? Certainly history shows the law is not hardened in concrete. So if we have had, and continue to have, innovation, then what does reliance on precedent mean?

It could be concluded, as Chief Justice Charles Evans Hughes said, that "the Constitution is what the judges say it is." But judges don't act in a vacuum. Studies of the people appointed to the federal courts show that they are mostly from highly privileged backgrounds. Not many mavericks, like a Louis D. Brandeis or a Thurgood Marshall, are appointed to the bench. Long ago one of Abraham Lincoln's appointees to the Supreme Court, Judge Samuel F. Miller, spoke frankly of the class bias of federal judges:

It is vain to contend with judges who have been at the bar, advocates for forty years of railroad companies, and all the forms of associated capital, when they are called upon to decide cases where such interests are in contest. All their training, all their feelings are from the start in favor of those who need no such influence.

The direction the Supreme Court takes depends partly on the political makeup of its majority. But even a conservative Court, under pressure from social upheaval, may realize it has to accept some reforms, if only to forestall a greater calamity. The Court, like all our institutions, is anchored in society. Its decisions are bound to reflect how the people at large think and feel, what they want, and what they cherish. Of course that "common will" of the people is complex and contradictory; it can shift unexpectedly and sometimes convulsively.

Over the years, a philosophy of "judicial restraint" has grown up that often seems to guide the Supreme Court. It was shaped in modern times by such judges as John Harlan, Learned Hand, and Felix Frankfurter. The conclusions they came to are summarized by the legal scholar Lincoln Caplan in this form:

The Supreme Court and other federal courts should defer when possible . . . to the judgments of democratically elected bodies, from the Congress down to local school boards. Since the states are the foundation of the Union, and the Constitution draws its power from them, the courts should defer to state and local over federal authority. Exercising passive virtues . . . courts should decide no case unnecessarily. When they do rule, they should do it on the narrowest possible grounds. Except in unusual instances, they should keep the law consistent and avoid rash decisions by closely following precedent. Judges should carefully interpret all sources of law, including cases, statutes, and the Constitution itself, and they should not read into a case or a law provisions that are not there.

What this speaks for is a nice blend of close analysis and common sense. Any change in the law should be carefully measured. Then, if sweeping social change requires innovative legal decision, the Court's ruling will be more acceptable.

The charge of "packing the Court" arises when a president has the duty of filling a vacancy on the bench. It is he who has the power of nominating a person to the federal courts but with the advice and consent of the Senate. The two have absolute equality in jointly constituting the Supreme Court. Every president tries to shape the Supreme Court to realize his own constitutional vision. But he can only try, not necessarily succeed.

When the Framers divided the appointment powers between the president and Senate (as they divided the treaty power), it was the result of one of the political compromises that made the Constitution possible. Ever since, ideology and politics have played a role in acceptance or rejection of nominees. Some nominees are turned down because they are too conservative, some because they are too liberal. Whether the Senate acts wisely or not, it is constitutionally entitled to do whatever it chooses as far as accepting or rejecting Supreme Court nominees. In the two centuries of our nation's history, one out of every five nominees has been turned down. Most constitutional experts agree that the social philosophy of judges shapes their decisions on the bench and, therefore, that philosophy is a proper factor in deciding a nominee's fitness to be a judge.

Parties and pressure groups do their utmost to exert influence on Supreme Court appointments. A furious debate erupted when in 1916 President Woodrow Wilson nominated the crusading liberal Louis D. Brandeis to the

Court. In 1987, when Robert Bork was nominated to the Court by President Ronald Reagan, Bork was assailed for views held to be too rigidly conservative. The Senate approved Brandeis, rejected Bork.

Interest groups and parties always seek to control the Supreme Court as they seek to control the Congress and the administrative agencies of government. Because the Court decides broad issues of public policy, it is the inevitable focus of pressure. Over the years, the Court can rarely keep to a position contrary to the views of a national majority. But meanwhile it can do damage to the policies the Court's majority does not favor.

Not long ago a rather novel view of the Supreme Court's authority was put forth by the then U.S. Attorney General, Edwin Meese, 3d. In speeches and articles he held that Supreme Court rulings are binding only on the parties to a particular ruling. He claimed that the Court does not decide what the law is except for individual cases. If his beliefs were applied to the *Brown v. Board of Education* decision, then only the school board involved would be obliged to bring about school integration. All other schools could remain segregated.

A broad criticism of Mr. Meese's position burst into print. Lawyers and constitutional authorities were appalled by his dictum that the Supreme Court's interpretations of the Constitution do "not establish a Supreme Law of the Land." No one, then, needs to obey a Supreme Court decision but the litigants—unless one feels like obeying it oneself. Tradition has always granted the last word on the law to the Court, unless of course an amendment to the Constitution is adopted.

Coming from the nation's chief law enforcement officer, it amazed many. But it was, said Meese's critics, a part of a systematic campaign to reinterpret and dismantle fundamental freedoms that the Constitution guarantees to all citizens. What he advocated seemed true to the Reagan Administration's conduct in many affairs: its Iran-Contra dealings, its failure to protect the environment or civil rights, its refusal to enforce federal statutes when they conflicted with the president's own moral and social ideas. As Lincoln Caplan wrote in the *New Yorker* magazine, "In grave, astonishing, and recurring actions, in both domestic and foreign affairs, the Administration has failed to enforce and obey the laws. It has repeatedly misinterpreted, circumvented, and defied the will of Congress.

"Unlike the Nixon Administration, which held that it was above the law," Caplan went on to say, "the Reagan Administration has in essence regularly proposed that it *is* the law."

The attitude of the White House toward the law can have a serious influence upon those in the administration whose duty it is to execute the law. In the Reagan years a climate of lawlessness was encouraged. Members of that administration ran up a record of misdeeds and illegal behavior that could not be matched in any administration before it. The *Washington Post* reported that between January 1981 and April of 1986, one hundred and ten senior Reagan officials were accused or found guilty of unethical or illegal conduct. This was months before the Iran-Contra affair leaked into the press, and before the Wedtech scandal broke, both of which implicated many more Reagan officials.

Lawyers know that law is not a science; it is an art. It can never be perfect, for it is the creation of imperfect people. Nor can it be truly neutral, for every issue of importance that comes to law is controversial. When law-making and law interpretations are done well and honestly, they contribute to the stability of society. They help make it possible for us to live in a more predictable world.

11

LOBBYISTS
AND
THOSE THEY SERVE

Lobbyist is a dirty word in many ears. One lobbyist has remarked, "When I say I'm a lobbyist, it's about the same as saying I'm a pimp." But how a lobbyist is seen often depends upon whose interests he or she serves. Most lobbyists are the spearheads of pressure groups. Whether they operate in Washington, D.C., a state capital, or a city hall, their business is to persuade people in government to act so as to benefit the clients the lobbyist serves.

In the nation's capital, it is estimated the army of lobbyists numbers about 11,000. The largest sector (about 3,750) are officers of the 1,900 trade and professional associations and labor unions with headquarters in Washington. Another 1,500 work for corporations. About the same number are advocates of special causes—environmental protection, prison reform, handgun control, saving whales, the equal rights amendment, and so forth.

Another 2,500 are lawyers and consultants registered as lobbyists or foreign agents who represent their clients in regulatory matters or legal problems with the government.

The lobbyists together with the great organized groups they represent are the "third house of Congress," or as one scholar puts it, an "invisible government." At one time they all had the smelly reputation of being unscrupulous, ready to use bribery or whatever means to achieve their goal. Today, however, lobbyists set out to get what they want pretty much in the open. Of course, sometimes corrupt deals are still made behind closed doors and reach public view only if an investigative reporter exposes it or an indictment is handed down.

The lobbyists have often had legislative or administrative experience in government. They know who's who and how to reach them. A survey made by the House Armed Services Committee found that more than 1,400 retired officers of the military, including 261 generals or admirals, had taken jobs with one or another of the 100 leading defense contractors. Their function as civilians was to lobby Congress and the bureaucracy to get business for their new bosses.

It's a sort of triangular trade, carried out in politics— from the defense contractors to the appropriate congressional committee to the Pentagon, and back down the line. The same thing goes on with many other triangles. Most often at the center is a group with a strong business interest at stake such as banking, manufacturing, trade, cotton, wheat, tobacco. The lobbyists dance back and forth between their interest group client, the bureaucrats, and the legislators, working out deals that benefit all three. The question is, How much, if at all, does the deal benefit the public?

It's not hard to see why the business world engages in such deals. Its prime purpose is to make profits and to survive. Government's role can be vital to the success or failure of their plans. Bureaucrats, too, want to survive. The government agencies need funding to do that, and to please clientele groups and legislators, they are likely to go along with what's asked of them by the powerful.

And the legislators? Their responsibility is to their constituents and the public at large. But it takes more and more money to get elected and reelected, as we've seen. PAC money is needed to finance their campaigns. Lobbyists for richly endowed interest groups are able to spread the money around, and it's hard to stay away from that pot of honey. In recent years much of the lobbying has gone into fund-raising. The lobbyists raise the money, and it buys them access to the legislators. That impresses their clients, who then give them still more money, which gains even more access. There's no end to it.

Sometimes lobbyists are on opposite sides of a legislative bill. Rather than fight each other to the death, they compromise. Behind the scenes they make a deal to work on Congress in such a way that everyone comes out with something—if not everything—gained. Often there are other groups of people, perhaps more numerous, who also have a stake in that bill. Nevertheless, if they are unorganized and without funds, they can't play in the game. There's no lobby to speak for them. Examining that factor the political scientist Harold Lasswell wrote,

"Those who get the most are *elite;* the rest are *mass.*"
No wonder *Fortune,* a leading business magazine, could
conclude that "the business community has been the most
effective special interest lobby in the country." It has "all
the primary instruments of power—the leadership, the
strategy, the supporting troops, the campaign money—
and a new will to use them."

Lobbyists for each interest group can always find friends
in the legislature. Every new legislator, like any political
reporter, quickly gets to know which members speak for
the banks, the oil companies, the tobacco growers, the
insurance firms, the physicians, the aged, the veterans,
and so on. The lobbyists do more than apply pressure
personally on that legislator. They organize pressure from
home, too. When a particular bill comes up, a stream of
letters, postcards, telegrams, petitions, and resolutions
from the home constituency floods the legislator's office.

A number of lobbies have achieved powerful influence
in Washington. One example is the leading pro-Israel
lobby, the American Israel Public Affairs Committee
(AIPAC). It is considered to be a major force in shaping
U.S. policy in the Middle East. According to the *New
York Times,* AIPAC has "gained the power to influence
a Presidential candidate's choice of staff, to block prac-
tically any arms sale to an Arab country and to serve as
a catalyst for intimate military relations between the Pentagon and the Israeli Army. Its leading officials are con-
sulted by State Department and White House policy makers,
by Senators and Generals."

The influence of AIPAC is the result of its skills in

lobbying both Congress and the executive branch. Members of Congress attribute its success to its simple coherent message and its single-minded devotion to a cause. While it doesn't itself endorse or give money to candidates, it influences many campaign contributions. The information it supplies Congress is held to be both timely and reliable. Finally, it has the advantage of a large number in Congress predisposed to help Israel; nearly half the members of both houses are consistent supporters of Israel.

How does a lobbyist for a nonprofit institution operate? Evelyn Dubrow, who has lobbied on Capitol Hill for some thirty years, is one of the most experienced veterans. Her boss is the International Ladies Garment Workers Union, and when she began roaming the halls of Congress for it, she was seeking support for a $1 minimum wage bill. A tiny woman with soft fluffy white curls, she learned not to pretend she knew all the answers. If you wing it, the legislator finds out and then distrusts you. She works fifteen-hour days, attends half a dozen political receptions in one night, and sometimes manages to buttonhole thirty senators in one day. She lobbies for such aims as a bill to broaden legislation against housing discrimination, another to bar discrimination in federally funded programs, or a provision in a trade bill to help protect America's textile, apparel, and shoe industries from unfair competition by imports.

Dubrow, the daughter of a union man, has worked for labor or liberal groups all her life. She doesn't believe in threatening members of Congress if they don't vote her way, nor does she ask for a vote as a personal favor. "Lobbying," she says, "is presenting your case and proving it."

A lobbyist such as Dubrow can't be lumped together with the corporate lobbyists. While labor unions can do important lobbying on job safety, a minimum wage, social security, health, education, and housing, they aren't in the same class as business in wielding influence. Some sources estimate the ratio is about ten to one in favor of business as a political force.

A younger lobbyist on Capitol Hill who works chiefly for nonprofit clients is Liz Robbins. She is a specialist in lobbying for federal aid on behalf of states and municipalities. Her career began with work for Senator Jacob Javits and New York's mayor, John Lindsay. A stint for the Department of Health, Education and Welfare followed, and then she opened a shop for herself. Although Robbins is not a lawyer, she nevertheless has several law firms among her clients. Her lobbying in Washington has helped save some states and cities millions and even billions of dollars. What you get for clients is often not the most important thing you do for them. What you save them can be just as important, she believes. Robbins has helped San Francisco secure federal funds to clean up San Francisco Bay. She also had rules redefined for Supplemental Security Insurance so that victims of acquired immune deficiency syndrome (AIDS) are allowed to receive benefits. Robbins is well established on the Hill, so she can pick and choose her clients. She prefers to work on those issues she finds personally involving, and has done pro bono work, too, for clients who can't afford a lobbyist.

The schedule of a lobbyist such as Robbins is frantic. She finds nothing glamorous about it; it's just hard work. In one week she may shuttle twice between Washington and New York, spend endless hours on the phone, and climb up and down the Hill to collar people in the House and Senate. She ignores no one on her path, believing everyone may be helpful—secretaries, doormen, waitresses, guards, and, of course, reporters. She carries a frequently sounding beeper everywhere she goes, even while playing softball in the country. In a dozen years on Capitol Hill, she has earned a reputation as a down-to-earth professional, the opposite of the glib wheeler-dealers whose machinations give lobbying a bad name.

That bad name made headlines in the late 1980s when a number of prominent political figures connected to the Reagan administration were investigated and tried for unethical or illegal practices in lobbying. In a cover story, *Time* magazine asked, "What ever happened to ethics?" The story noted:

More than 100 members of the Reagan Administration have had ethical or legal charges leveled against them. That number is without precedent. While the Reagan Administration's missteps may not have been as flagrant as the Teapot Dome scandal, or as pernicious as Watergate, they seem more general, more pervasive and somehow more ingrained than those of any previous Administration. During other presidencies, scandals such as Watergate seemed to multiply from a single cancer; the Reagan Administration, however, appears to have suffered a breakdown of the immune system, opening the way to all kinds of ethical and moral infections.

To give but one example: an extensive investigation into the Wedtech Corporation, a South Bronx military contractor, led to many indictments. The Wedtech case proved to be the largest dollar scandal in U.S. government history. A lobbyist for the company pleaded guilty to using corrupt practices in representing Wedtech at the White House and with federal agencies and law-enforcement officials. He admitted offering a $10,000 bribe in cash to "supplement the income" of an officer of the Small Business Administration. At the time, Wedtech was seeking a $134 million contract to make portable pontoons for the Navy. Another man, the former head of New York's state militia, admitted taking a $58,000 bribe from Wedtech to lobby the federal government for military contracts for the company.

Wedtech's corporate counsel said half a dozen consultants with strong political connections received nearly $5 million. Reagan's Attorney General, Edwin Meese, himself came under investigation in the Wedtech case, to determine whether he used his official position for personal profit. Wedtech "won a major military contract after Mr. Meese, who later became profitably associated with one of its directors, had strongly interceded in its behalf," according to the New York Times.

Through this period Wedtech also courted Democratic officials—the Bronx Borough President, Stanley Simon, Congressman Mario Biaggi, and others—rewarding them in one form or another for using their political influence in lobbying for the company. Over the years Wedtech hired more than a dozen influential consultants (read lob-

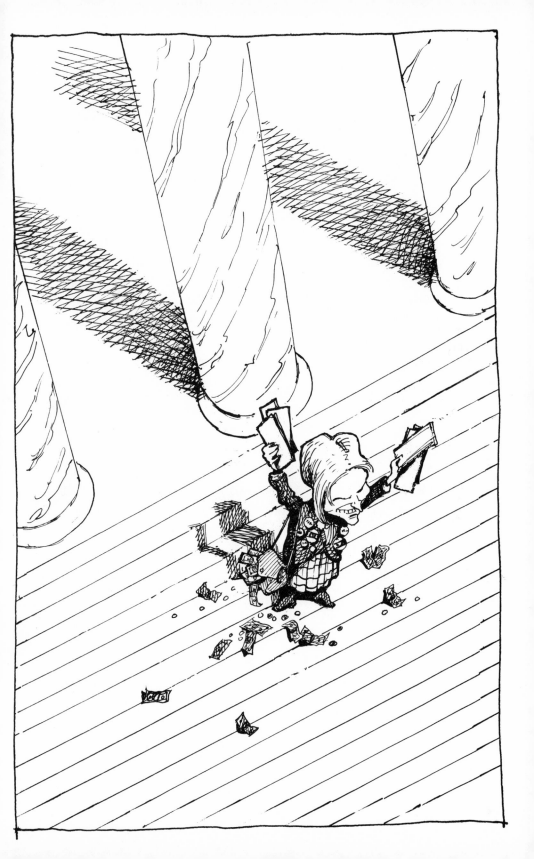

byists), including retired generals and a former Secretary of the Air Force.

The direct payoff in cash is the old crude way of wielding influence, but it hasn't gone altogether out of style. Corporate lobbyists nowadays have more refined methods of providing rewards for favors. They can arrange handsome lecture fees, promise high-paying jobs in private industry, throw lavish parties, and offer luxurious vacation trips. The cynical billionaire Howard Hughes once told an associate, "Everyone has a price." He handed out nearly half a million a year to "councilmen and county supervisors, tax assessors, sheriffs, state senators and assemblymen, district attorneys, governors, congressmen and senators, judges—yes, and vice presidents and presidents, too."

The Speaker of the House for ten years, Thomas ("Tip") O'Neill, once said, "The grab of special interests is staggering. It will destroy the legislative process." The work of one lobbyist alone, who operated twelve years, demonstrates the danger. According to federal investigators, Claude Wild, Jr., lobbying for Gulf Oil, handed out over $4 million of Gulf's money to about 100 members of Congress, 18 governors, and scores of judges and local politicians. Four presidents accepted gifts from him. No one was ever prosecuted.

So money talks in every aspect of American politics. Lobbyists spend millions of hours and dollars a year to make the world comfortable for their clients. Their influence outweighs public opinion. Lobbyists can see that a single bill gets adopted, or even a whole package of legislation, while the public has no idea what the lobbyists are doing. Perhaps the public would be strongly opposed to the result if only they knew about it. Lobbyists for big business have succeeded, for example, in lowering tax rates so that just one private interest, the oil industry, saves about $9 billion. This was done while tax rates for the lower-income groups have gone up.

Many Americans join no interest group. Research shows that about 25 percent of the people belong to no group at all, not even a church. They surely have common interests in some respects, including the basic desire to stay alive and live decently. But when people want something, they don't always join together to get it. The poorest, who rarely have the information, the time, or the money, are least likely to join a group to defend their interests. Who are their lobbyists?

12

BUREAUCRATS AND WHISTLE-BLOWERS

President George Washington's first task in office was to appoint officials to run the new government's departments. In the beginning there were only five executive departments, led by an attorney general, a postmaster general, and the secretaries of state, treasury, and war. From time to time as the expanding business of government required, Congress added new executive departments and agencies. Today there are thirteen departments represented in the president's cabinet and scores of federal agencies to carry on the work of government. By 1988 the United States employed nearly 3 million civilians in the executive departments and the independent agencies. The largest number, about 1 million, are in the Defense Department; the next largest, some 700,000, in the Postal Service; and next, about 240,000, in the Veterans Administration. The president's executive office alone has about 1,600 employees.

No modern government can function without such support. The army of bureaucrats (as they are called) is needed to regulate the affairs of a highly complex, centralized society with all the demands it makes upon the state. Similar bureaucracies, on a smaller scale, handle the business of state and local governments. These agencies do more than carry out policies decided upon by the legislature. They also have a hand in the formation of public policy. Each department or agency serves some section of the society, and at times it speaks for that segment before the legislature and to the public at large. Most agencies carry out research to determine public needs and suggest government action. When budgets are in the making, the departments and agencies lobby to maintain their programs or expand it.

In many ways agencies are much like the pressure groups already discussed. They, too, operate upon the legislature to advance their interests and frequently collaborate with private groups when they share a common purpose. So the bureaucracy does not exist apart from politics. Agencies negotiate, make deals, and reach compromises to get as much as possible to satisfy their needs. True, election results may redirect their efforts, but rarely are they tossed out of power.

The agencies' power is considerable. If you put all the administrative services of government—federal, state, and local—together, they would far outweigh the biggest corporations. That the agencies have grown so much and so rapidly is due to the highly specialized nature of modern society. Take our food supply. No service is more essential. When farmers raised food products and sold them directly to the local market, government played no role. But then an enormous division of labor developed in the supply of food to a national and international market. In a thousand different places farmers raise crops that are then transported to many plants where they are processed and distributed to wholesalers and retailers for purchase by the consumer. To ensure the purity and safety of the food supply, legislatures passed many laws and set up various agencies that monitor the elaborate operations. The goal is to see that consumers get honest value for their dollar and are not injured by the product.

Some services, essential though they may be, would not be provided at all if government did not undertake them. For when no profit seems possible, private business is not interested. Government steps in, using its power to tax; government raises the money and hires the people to perform the service.

The value of a skilled corps of government workers is obvious. They strengthen any state when they do not become so entrenched and conservative that they block progress. Governments of all political shades rely on their bureaucracies. Little would get done without them. But sometimes little gets done *because* of them. It doesn't matter what a reform on paper says if the people in the agencies aren't willing to put it into effect. The president (or a department head) issues orders, but if the staff down below aren't convinced it's a good thing, or at least good for *them*, little will get done.

Are the bureaucratic agencies of government neutral? Nonpolitical? The truth is that politics does not stop at the agency's door. Bureaucrats are subject to the pressure of interest groups. Which laws or regulations they apply and which they ignore, what interpretations they give, what actions they take are of great concern to lobbyists. Their clients profit greatly or lose greatly by what the bureaucracy does.

Agencies make innumerable rulings, decisions that often have the strength of law. In one case, for example, a federal commission approved a $2 billion rate rise for 110 telephone, gas, and electric companies. Thus, without legislative approval, the agency laid a heavy burden on the public. The agency had become hostage to the industry it was supposed to regulate. But who knew what was going on?

This can happen, too, in the case of agencies designed to protect the public well-being. One example is the Occupational Safety and Health Administration (OSHA). Since the early 1970s, OSHA has been charged with protecting the health and safety of tens of millions of workers in the nation's 5 million work places. Understaffed and underfunded, OSHA moves slowly when it decides to act, and it has lacked enforcement tools. OSHA was originally meant to be an enforcement body; in the Reagan years it saw itself more as a partner of business. Reagan attacked OSHA for burdening companies with overly technical regulations, and Reagan staffers changed the rules to exempt many employers from inspection. Worker injuries and illnesses began to jump. OSHA even failed to keep close track of accidents that kill workers on the job.

Fines imposed for safety violations are so small that companies pay them readily and go right on breaking the
rules.

A long struggle for a drink of water is a simple example
of the difficulty of making OSHA do its job properly.
Until 1987, farm workers were the only workers not assured access to basic sanitary facilities. They were not
entitled to wash their hands, drink fresh water, or relieve
themselves in toilets while at work. It took fourteen years
of bitter debates and court actions to get OSHA to approve such a rule. Finally in 1987 an appeals court re-
buked OSHA for resisting the necessity. But even with a
rule in place, OSHA was accused of doing as little as
possible to insure that employers would abide by the rule.
Union safety experts held that the agency had "essentially
no program to protect workers in any field." According
to international data, more Americans die at work than
do their counterparts in many other countries.

When something seems so bad that honest public servants cannot stand it, they may tell a reporter or a member
of Congress about it. In 1987 employees of the Nuclear
Regulatory Commission (NRC) publicly accused the agency
of favoring the nuclear power industry at the cost of
public safety. Staffers testified before a House group on
nuclear oversight that the agency's top staff director had
thwarted safety regulations, altered a fire safety program
after meeting privately with industry representatives, and
acceded to one industry request not to impose a drug and
alcohol code on reactor workers. This was corroborated
when one of the NRC's five commissioners, James K.
Asseltine, resigned in 1987. He said that the level of safety

at nuclear reactors around the country was so low that a fatal meltdown in the next ten to twenty years would not be a surprise.

Such public criticism defies the code of secrecy bureaucracy cherishes, and the "whistle-blower" risks grave punishment. Bureaucracies tend to shield themselves from public criticism by hiding the facts. When secrecy is challenged, say by Congress or the press, officials may not hesitate to lie. Both the Watergate and the Iran-Contra scandals gave ample evidence of a readiness to lie to cover up the truth. Public officials on high levels lied to the Congress and to the public about their illegal covert actions when forced to face investigations.

Several administrations have concealed the U.S. role in overthrowing popular governments in countries like Guatemala, Indonesia, Iran, and Chile, to name but a few. The government lied to keep secret the bombing raids that devastated Cambodia during 1969 and 1970. When a Senate committee looked into such matters, it estimated the United States had some 500 secret agreements with other countries that the White House had never revealed to the Congress.

If whistle-blowers disclose the truth, it may cost them their job. The case of Ernest Fitzgerald was one of the rare ones to reach public attention. When Fitzgerald worked for the Air Force as an analyst of weapons costs, he testified that a Lockheed cargo plane cost the country $2 billion more than contracted for. He was fired by the Air Force. He spent thirteen years in courts before he won reinstatement in 1982. Fitzgerald, a folk hero to other whistle-blowers, warns that doing it is like "setting your house on fire publicly."

As a result of public anger over Fitzgerald's fate, a special board was set up to give protection to government workers who report discrimination, mismanagement, and corruption. Within four months a thousand complaints came in. But the board applied the law in a way that gave whistle-blowers even less protection. It placed the burden of investigating and proving complaints on the whistle-blower, rather than on the agency.

Whistle-blowers are in danger on the local level, too. In New York, Herb Rosenblum discovered 14,000 phantoms enrolled in the city Medicare program. He didn't get a raise, but was demoted by the Human Resources Administration. When Irwin Levin disclosed that nine children had died at least in part because of negligence in New York City's Special Services for Children program, his reward was suspension and a fine.

A popular lament is that bureaucracy is so choked by red tape that nothing seems to get done, whether it's in municipal, state, or federal government. It only appears to be so. Some things are done quickly; others slowly, if at all. Why? Because action often depends on the power of the groups behind the law. Presumably all laws Congress adopts have equal standing. However, what happened to a law that set up a medical care program for poor children, shows otherwise. The law made about 13 million children eligible for medical examination and treatment. Years after the law was adopted, only about 15 percent of the children had been examined. It meant, said a congressional subcommittee, the "unnecessary crippling, retardation, or even death of thousands of children." Enforcement was neglected because the poor have no power in Washington. Yet when a multibillion-dollar, high-profit weapons system is put into the works by Congress, the vast project goes into high gear at once. Defense contractors, the Pentagon, the many members of Congress whose districts will get fat contracts, and the research centers whose budgets will be swelled all combine their political influence to reap the benefits of the law.

When it comes to enforcing a law *against* the poor and the powerless, bureaucracy manages to move fast. Every time eligibility rules are tightened for the people dependent on federal aid, the cuts are made swiftly.

Of course, there is considerable waste of federal funds because of the huge size and complexity of the bureaucracy. In 1983 the Grace Commission concluded that $141 billion could be saved each year by cutting government bureaucratic waste. One agency, for example, makes a study of mass transportation problems, only to find out later that two other agencies had already done the same thing. There may be a dozen advisory committees on cancer and a dozen agencies dealing with consumer issues. Waste and duplication are a curse in so vast a government administration as ours. Once an agency is established it is apparently very hard to reshape it or remove it.

How big an agency is in manpower and budget does not indicate how effective it will be in serving the country's needs. Much depends on the power of those who command its services. As we know, the unorganized and the needy often fail to get what they should from the agencies concerned. Yet when it came to landing astronauts on the moon—a gigantic task of coordination—the bureaucracies concerned proved enormously capable. They had the right political support.

So in looking at how bureaucracies function, the question to consider is, Why do they perform so well in some cases and so badly in others?

13

MUCKRAKERS AND MILLIONAIRES

When Great Britain gave up its thirteen American colonies, they set about recreating themselves as independent states. At the same time, they had to establish a new central government to deal with their common interests. The first goal was more important than the second because state governments in those times had more effect on everyday life than did the national government. In place of the old colonial charters, the people wrote constitutions setting out the system of government they wanted and the powers that government would have. The constitutions, pretty much alike, established three divisions of government: an elected legislature to write the laws, an executive to carry them out, and courts to interpret the laws.

There were some differences among the state constitutions, but they were all basically democratic. The people made the rules they wanted to be governed by; the government officials would be their servants, not their masters. The people created their constitutions peacefully, though with plenty of fierce argument, and provided for them to be changed by orderly, legal means. In devising the new system, the people of the states debated hotly the same central issue that would come to the fore later in the Constitutional Convention at Philadelphia. Some groups feared government would be dominated by the aristocrats, the men of wealth and power. Other groups feared control by the far more numerous poor—the artisans and manual laborers of the towns. The constitutions were a compromise that sought to protect private property while preventing the rich from using their influence against the other classes of society.

At the Constitutional Convention in 1787, the states might have chosen to abolish themselves in favor of a national government that would take all power into its hands. That was hardly likely, for the states considered themselves the foundation of the American nation. It was the states that selected the delegates who got together to write a new Constitution better able to meet the common needs of the Union of states.

It was the beginning of what is called the federalist system. The states retained much power, although they could not leave the Union at will. (The Civil War settled that question.) To the central government went certain powers, but not a monopoly of power. This division of power between the two levels of government—state and federal—was intended to ensure the stability of the American system.

American political conditions did not get much close scrutiny for almost a hundred years. Between the end of the Civil War and the close of the nineteenth century the nation's business and industrial life was transformed. There was an explosion of material development. Whole systems of industry and whole regions of industrial production were created. The urban population multiplied three times, and the larger cities expanded at such a dizzying rate that their growth outstripped government's ability to manage it.

By 1900 some Americans began to realize that all this material growth had been achieved at a terrible cost. Human values were trampled underfoot and natural resources destroyed. Both the land and the people were robbed. Men, women, and children were treated as things to produce more things. When their working strength was exhausted, they were flung aside. Farmers got pathetic returns for their harsh toil. The cities grew into industrial wastelands—grim, ugly, crowded, reeking of crime and poverty, and administered so corruptly that democracy became a joke.

"Business, great and small," wrote the historian Richard Hofstadter, "had debased politics: working with powerful bosses in city, state, and nation, it had won favors and privileges in return for its subsidies to corrupt machines. Domination of affairs by political bosses and business organizations was now seen to be a threat to democracy itself."

How did business control politics? The midwestern journalist William Allen White described the operations of the old boss system in city government:

Muckrakers and Millionaires • 131

The extra-constitutional place of the boss in government was as the extra-constitutional guardian of business. If a telephone company desired to put poles in the street, and the city council objected, straightway went the owner of the telephone stock to the boss. He straightened matters out. If a street car company was having trouble with the city street department, the manager of the street railway went to the boss, and the street department became reasonable. . . . Always business was considered. . . . Money in politics was there for the purpose of protecting the rights of property under the law, as against the rights of men. The greed of capital was rampant, the force of democracy was dormant.

The slime spread upward, reaching into the state and national capitals. White shows how it worked to benefit the railroads:

Railroads, being the most important public service corporations in any state, had the closest relations with the state bosses who controlled members of the legislature, so the legal departments of the railroads named United States Senators. In those days in many of the states a candidate for United States senator usually went to the law departments of the railroads in his state, and made his peace. Otherwise he was defeated. Now, man is a grateful brute, and when federal judges were to be named, the law departments of the railroads generally had a judicial candidate in view. And the senator whose business it is to nominate federal judges for the President of the United States to appoint, subject to the Senate's confirmation, generally chose the man who was satisfactory to the powers in his state that made him senator. As there are two sides to every lawsuit, whenever the interests of the public and the interests of the railroad clashed in court, it was as easy to see the railroad's side as it was to see the other side, so the mass of federal decisions for years favored the railroads. . . .

What had happened? The mass mobilization of the nation's productive energy had wiped out moral energy. The nation had failed to develop ways to meet human needs or to control the harm done by such rapid physical change. But men and women of goodwill, no longer heedless of the corruption and waste, began trying to nurse moral concern into life, to examine the behavior of business and industry, and to seek ways to halt political corruption and restore democracy to the citizens.

By 1900 there were so many thinking this way that they became a movement called the Progressives. This movement was greatly helped by a group of journalists who played a vital role in the national awakening. The work of these muckrakers, as they were called, appeared in several magazines of mass circulation and in popular books. They wrote about what was actually going on in American business and politics. They named names and places and went beyond that to point out what was wrong with the whole of American society. It was tough, unsentimental, factual reporting, the forerunner of the investigative journalism that would do so much to expose social and political evils from the 1960s on.

The Progressives had no single blueprint for a better society. They differed from each other in many ways. But all wanted to see the promise of American life fulfilled for the masses of the people. They did everything they could to spread information about injustice and inequality and to urge citizens to use the ballot to change things. They raised many issues: monopolies, taxation, conditions of labor, woman suffrage, the rights of blacks.

The movement began in the cities, spread quickly to

the states, and then reached the national level. It made great gains in the 1890s, reforming the governments of Chicago, Detroit, Milwaukee, New York, and other cities. Scores of middle-class citizen groups organized to work for betterment of local conditions. What soon became clear was that city government was often at the mercy of state control. Many of the abuses to be remedied could be reached only by state action. So the reformers had to tackle state legislators who were frequently allies of city bosses. Yet the reformers managed to make political progress in the state capitals. They did it so well that several of them were elected state governors: Robert M. La Follette in Wisconsin, Hiram Johnson in California, Charles Evans Hughes in New York, Woodrow Wilson in New Jersey, James Cox in Ohio. Once in office, they fought hard battles to regulate business, introduce social reforms, and end corrupt practices.

It was a democratic revolt, a movement of diverse people doing their best to make politics work in the interests of all, not just the privileged few. The measures they put forth called for a more direct popular role in government and for reforms that would break the grip of political bosses and put government into the hands of the people.

The movement succeeded in getting many states to adopt reforms. The *direct primary* was meant to give the people, rather than the party machines, the right to choose political candidates. The *initiative* gave citizen groups the opportunity to propose legislation. The *referendum* made it possible for voters to reconsider and revoke state laws. The *recall of public officials* was designed to get rid of corrupt or incompetent officials before their term of office ended. The *corrupt practices acts* were tools to pry apart the illegal ties between money and politics. The *public recall of judges* was intended to remove judges whose rulings were corruptly influenced.

Reform reached into national affairs too. The Senate itself, long known as the "Millionaires Club" (two-thirds of whose members were said to be the direct agents of the moneyed interests), was changed by the reform movement when the 17th Amendment (1913) took the power to appoint senators away from the state legislatures and required that senators be chosen in direct elections by the people.

Not every reform proved effective. Enforcement depended upon the vigilance of the public and its willingness to keep fighting for democratic change. The mood of the Progressive era did not endure; no popular tide of feeling can persist very long. With the opening of the 1920s, the movement petered out. People were tired of the struggle, frustrated by the stubborn resistance reform always meets.

The reform movement never affected the maldistribution of wealth in the United States. It became even more concentrated than before. A report by a federal commission under President Wilson said:

The Rich, 2 percent of the people, own 35 percent of the wealth. The Poor, 65 percent of the people, own 5 percent of the wealth. The largest private fortune in the U.S., estimated at one billion dollars, is equivalent to the aggregate wealth of 2,500,000 of those who are classed as Poor, who are shown to own on the average about $400 each.

(Is that inequality any less enormous today? The richest 5 percent of Americans now receive more income than the bottom 40 percent. The richest 1 percent own more assets than the bottom 90 percent, according to the economist David M. Kotz at the University of Massachusetts.)

Nor did the Progressives succeed in regulating business effectively. Federal or state agencies set up to protect the public interest often became the tools of the private interests they were supposed to police. While the devices created to check bossism remained on the books and helped limit corruption, that kind of politician managed to retain power by one means or another. There was a Boss Tweed in New York, a Boss Hague in New Jersey, a Boss Daley in Chicago, and other bosses like them who manipulated politics for decades and even generations.

Still, the reform movement had a lasting effect for the way it encouraged political criticism and raised social consciousness. It made Americans suspicious of big business and the special interests and more alert to practices that distorted political life. The country came out of that era believing that government has a great responsibility for the welfare of all its citizens, including the poor, the weak, and the silent.

When the Reagan administration came to power in 1981, the new president promised "to curb the size and influence of the federal establishment." During his two terms he did redistribute some power from the federal government to the states—mostly by cutting the budgets and staffs of various agencies, such as those providing welfare, Medicaid, food stamps, environmental protection, civil rights enforcement. At the same time, he vastly increased defense spending. Instead of balancing the budget, as he had promised, President Reagan ran up the biggest budget deficit in American history.

His program was at first welcomed by many because it tapped a popular dislike for a huge bureaucracy and satisfied a desire to see greater control of our affairs brought closer to home. The trouble with the new federalism in practice, however, was that state budgets were in poor shape because of periods of economic recession. If the federal government didn't provide the authority and budget to enforce civil rights, for instance, the state governments could do little about it. The effect was to let many essential services wither or die, and that, some Reagan critics charged, was just what he intended.

No one doubts that the role of the states in government has declined over the long span of time. But that is largely the result of great changes in American life—the irresistible growth of industrial power and of a tightly integrated international economy and the development of social and economic problems that can only be handled on a national scale. It still leaves room for the states to conduct much public business on their own and even to experiment imaginatively, as many have in recent years, in various fields such as education, child care, and economic development. As governors gain more power from their state legislatures, the public demands that they use it to try to solve economic and social problems.

Sometimes, the push for greater states' rights is used as a cover for something else. The White House may cry states' rights on one issue and call for the opposite on another. Often the position taken has much to do with

special interest pressure. Federalism is invoked by conservatives, and liberals too, as it suits their purpose, to
achieve a political goal.

Business often prefers to rely on state power because
its connections with the state political machine are more
intimate. Business lobbyists can use their influence in the
state legislature to block undesirable bills or at least to
prevent their effective administration. The lobbyists swear
no allegiance to any one party. They will place their money
on whichever party dominates the state government,
whether it be Democratic or Republican.

In *Boss,* his book about Chicago mayor Richard J.
Daley, Mike Royko describes the shady operations of the
Illinois state legislature some years back. Lobbyists expected to pay for votes, he said, and "their generosity
was matched by the legislators' greed. . . . Everybody knew
the next man's appetites and his price."

Such corruption in state and city politics goes back a
long way as we've seen. It has been vividly described by
such writers as Ida Tarbell, Upton Sinclair, and Lincoln
Steffens. Just as flamboyant are the practices of many
state politicians today. In Alaska, Lewis Discher, one of
the most influential figures in state politics, was indicted
in 1987 on charges of bribery, extortion, income tax fraud,
and accepting kickbacks while doing business as both
lobbyist and construction executive. The government said
he took some $9 million in bribes and kickbacks from
companies that wanted business deals with his county.

The nation's media have little trouble unearthing similar examples of the influence of private interests upon
public affairs. Some things that make corruption easier

are built into the system itself. Men and women who sit in most city councils or state legislatures are part-time public officials. They also run a law practice or a business and often have to weigh government decisions against the interests of their law clients or business associates.

Take a New York state senator whose law firm is paid $175,000 a year to represent a utility's interests. Such questions as rate hikes or exemptions from using certain fuels are issues he has to vote on. Or look at the staff counsel for a legislative committee. In Albany one such man gets $60,000 a year to advise a housing committee and at the same time is a member of a law firm that represents landlords in disputes with tenants. Another counsel is a partner in a law firm that represents motor carriers. That man helped draft the deregulation of the trucking industry.

The two top Republican leaders in the New York Senate are part of a law firm representing many corporate clients, including banking, insurance companies, and utilities. Both men consistently back legislation benefiting their clients. Among the 211 legislators and the vast army of 5,000 people on the legislature's payroll one finds many similar links to private interests.

In some states, ethics codes have been adopted to set standards; they require greater financial disclosure and attempt to curb conflicts of interest. Many citizens believe legislatures should convert from part-time to full-time, prohibiting outside business and law activities by its members.

As the influence of party leaders fades, legislative leaders and their staffs move in to fill the gap. They run extensive campaigns and fund-raising activities for the members. This concentrates a great amount of power in a few hands. The chance for corruption increases. Lawmakers are more prone to do as they are told by the leaders. Putting no-show employees on the payroll becomes a way to get free help in running campaigns.

The grip a tightly held leadership has on the New York legislature makes for two worlds in Albany, the state capital. One operates behind the scenes and the other is just theater for the public. In civics textbooks the diagrams of the legislative process have little to do with what goes on behind the scenes. In 1987 an Albany reporter for the *New York Times* observed:

Usually only bills the leadership wants to pass are brought to the floor for debate and vote, so any bill being debated is virtually assured of passage. With some exceptions, the debate—although its contents are sincere and sometimes emotional—is really part theater, generating quotations for the news media and for newsletters to constituents.

Far to the south, that same year, forty-five county officials in Mississippi were indicted—and most pleaded guilty—for accepting kickbacks, for extortion, and for mail fraud. They took kickbacks from contractors or equipment suppliers in return for doing business with their companies. The same crimes were charged against public officials in New York and Georgia. In Oklahoma in 1981 an FBI investigation resulted in the conviction of 175 of the state's 231 elected county officials. The result brought about a saving of nearly 50 percent in the cost of providing county services in Oklahoma. On a single corrupt deal officials would net from $50 to $5,000, lining their pockets at the taxpayers' expense.

In many places the creation of "public authorities" has permitted high state officials to wheel and deal outside of public scrutiny. The Thruway Authority is but one of 99 such creations in New York State, the chairmen of which all have great power. They are appointed by the politicians they helped put in the governor's chair. Some seventy authority employees in the state are each paid more than the $100,000 a year the governor himself receives. Operating almost on their own, they become focal points of corruption. Phony employees are added to the payroll, multimillion dollar consulting contracts are given out in no-bid deals. In 1987 the authority's two top officials were forced to resign by scandals. As one state assemblyman said, "The Thruway Authority has been a dumping ground for political hacks, for both Democratic and Republican Administrations. Coupled with the fact that there has been virtually no oversight, it's not surprising that scandals would occur."

14

THE COST
OF CORRUPTION

In 1986 the biggest corruption scandal in 50 years made headlines in the New York press. A complex investigation into bribery was launched and continued for years. But it was a story not unique to New York. Corruption was happening, too, in Chicago, Syracuse, Boston, Philadelphia, and Washington. Public officials betrayed public trust to profit illegally from their public office.

In Chicago, a federal investigation into corruption in Cook County's court system resulted in sixty-five indictments and fifty-five convictions for bribery schemes. More than 120 Chicago-area officials, village mayors, sheriffs, deputies, and state representatives were also indicted on corruption charges. In Washington, D.C., two deputy mayors were sent to jail for steering contracts to friends in exchange for kickbacks, and nine other officials were convicted of crimes. In Philadelphia, a succession of special grand jury investigations all exposed pervasive corruption; none managed to stamp it out. A law professor directing a task force study of graft in the city's police force said Philadelphians believe "investigators come and go but corruption abideth." In Syracuse, a mayor who served the city for sixteen years and was elected president of the U.S. Conference of Mayors pleaded guilty in 1988 to charges of masterminding a scheme that brought him $1.5 million in kickbacks from city contractors. He was sentenced to ten years in prison.

Why did it happen? How could politicians in so many places break the trust between citizens and those who serve them? To many observers it was a sign of cities so deeply in trouble that corruption had become an inevitable part of political life. Rudolph Giuliani, the U.S. Attorney who prosecuted many New York politicians, said that "the practice of politics in this city stinks. People easily learn that the way to do things is through bribery . . . to pay money, to give favors, and not to try to get things done on the merits."

Giuliani's investigations led to the indictments of over three dozen City Hall regulars and people in the private sector accused of being their partners in corruption. Several were convicted on charges of having turned a city agency into a racketeering enterprise for their own enrichment. The agency—the Parking Violations Bureau (PVB)—brought in more money than any other source except taxes. In 1986 it issued a million tickets and took in $175 million. The PVB case involved two of the top Democratic leaders in New York: Donald Manes, the borough president of Queens, and Stanley Friedman, the

Democratic leader in the Bronx. Both men were close friends and political allies of Mayor Edward Koch. They ran the PVB as a criminal enterprise, stealing, rigging contracts, and systematically corrupting a major city agency. The editor of the *New York Daily News* said such corruption had been "going on for several years, and there are people out there right now with their pockets full who are never going to get caught."

Manes, who committed suicide before being brought to trial, had tremendous weight in politics. He also sat on the Board of Estimate, which decides on most contracts affecting the city and his own borough. As Queens party boss, he decided who would be a judge, who would get jobs, and who would get favors. He was a force in national politics because he could deliver the votes in a borough of 2 million people. His endorsement was eagerly sought by candidates for the presidency of the United States.

The system used was simple. The collections agencies under contract to the city pursued people with unpaid parking tickets. As their commission, the companies kept a percentage of the money they collected. The officials of the PVB demanded kickbacks for doing business with the agency, and the politicians pocketed the cash. It was like any protection racket, where some two-bit thug threatens to throw rocks through a neighborhood store window unless the owner pays protection money regularly. But it's even uglier when the politicians in power, who are supposed to protect people, steal from them instead.

The corruption is chronic, said political reporter Jack

Newfield. It afflicts one-party cities like New York, Chicago, Boston, Philadelphia, and Camden, New Jersey. The big-city political machines, once thought dead, are still durable and adaptable. He described the New York machine as:

> an infrastructure of permanent institutions. It contains law firms, landlords who make contributions, judges who channel judicial patronage to clubhouse lawyers, printing companies that get all the petition and literature business, community newspapers that receive judicial advertising, and friendly unions. In the Bronx, it controls the community school boards and picks principals on the basis of politics, not education. . . . The machine is rooted in the values of power and greed, just as Wall Street is rooted in the values of greed and power. The inside traders in both subcultures are natural products of their environment.

After the convictions of Friedman and the others indicted with him, Giuliani said such men proceed from the assumption that they are in office "to cash in on their political power." They want "as much money as they can get their hands on." How do they justify such behavior? Selwyn Rabb, a *New York Times* reporter who covered the story, said they make excuses for their greed by telling themselves they're "underappreciated and underpaid." They see themselves as making great sacrifices by their hard work for the party and the government. They feel entitled to certain rewards others might see as unethical but which they consider part of the system. "What's wrong with giving a job to a relative? What's wrong with getting a contract for a friend? What's wrong with, after being a regulator, going out to work for the company that you regulated?" They don't consider what they do as that venal.

David Zornow, another U.S. prosecutor of the criminal conspirators, sees them this way:

When you are a politician and you've been around for a long time, and you're reelected time after time with so overwhelming a percentage of the vote, when you run a political organization that is peopled with minions who are willing to do your bidding, and who live in large part to support the organization and support the county leader, it provides a person with a tremendous sense of ego, of standing above it all, of believing that you cannot get caught and that you're really larger than life. That's something that poisoned Donald Manes and Stanley Friedman. . . . I believe they thought they were powerful and important enough so that no one would find out.

That scandal opened the door to a host of other investigations in New York. During 1986 and 1987 the commissioners of Hospitals, Taxis, Transportation, Cultural Affairs, and Business Development, two members of the City Planning Commission, a borough president, and a U.S. congressman all resigned or were indicted. Said Jack Newfield, "The crime rate among party bosses in New York—50%—is now higher than for any other identifiable grouping in the world." The corruption seeped down to lower levels. More than half of the city's sewer inspectors, almost half of the electrical inspectors, and a quarter of the housing superintendents were arrested for graft.

People asked, Is there something in the very nature of our cities that makes it easier for corruption to flourish? Have big cities lost the sense of community, of human connectedness, that exists in small places? (But towns and villages, too, have their share of corruption.) Does the whole American society foster self-interest, self-centeredness? Are Americans so driven to make it, to be number one, that they will do it at any cost?

What keeps the machine in power in New York, adds Newfield, is "the combination of a docile press, an ineffective reform movement, and a moribund Republican Party." State legislatures tend to block the funding of independent commissions to probe the root causes of corruption scandals. Their members want to protect their own business interests. Little is done by city or state to combat systemic club patronage, which gets around civil service laws, to protect whistle-blowers, or to reform the systems of letting contracts. Few politicians are eager to ban party leaders from doing business with government or from the holding of elective office.

But corruption in the narrow sense of buying and selling political favors is only one aspect of city politics going bad. Consider what happens to a great city when the profit-making needs of the rich and the powerful dictate municipal policy. Again, New York will serve as the horrible example. In recent years, the city's biggest real-estate developers—the Trumps, Helmsleys, Lefraks, Macklowes—bought enormous influence at City Hall. They made huge contributions to Mayor Koch's election campaigns and won the inside track to make radical changes in the city's physical and political shape. Without the people ever being asked what they wanted their city to be like, the Koch administration and the developers rushed ahead to do great harm to the city.

Marshall Brown, a political scientist, describes the result:

New Yorkers are apt to wake up and find that the streets and buildings around them have been demolished in the middle of the night, to be rebuilt as reservations for the rich. The unkindest cut is that thanks to Koch's tax exemption and abatement policies we are subsidizing the destruction of our neighborhoods with our own tax money. The big developers and their satellites have been given hundreds of millions in public funds to build immensely profitable headquarters, luxury housing and amenities for private capital. They are exploiting New York like a gold mine and treating its people and its environment as so much slag, to be drained off when we get in the way.

What does corruption cost us, the citizens? It has a direct impact upon our lives. Revenues that should go to the city for the benefit of all are instead stolen, wasted, or lost. We pay more for services, not less, because a small number of people get rich upon our dollars. When the real-estate industry gains access to a mayor with political contributions, they get in exchange approvals of land assemblage, zoning variances, tax abatements, leases. Then they put up many huge buildings, displacing residents and small businesses, reducing or spoiling our light and air, and destroying our neighborhoods. It is the speculators who determine the income and racial composition of whole communities.

Corruption in government costs us in loss of quality in public staffs. Patronage prevents a city from getting the best staff possible. Instead, jobs are filled with pals and family and political hacks. These people are less likely to raise questions about contracts or complain of mismanagement. Patronage spoils the reputation of public service. The people assume others go into government only for what they can get out ot it, not because it is an honorable profession. Good people quit their government jobs because they don't want to be tainted by the atmosphere of corruption. Why stick to work that no longer commands respect?

Damage is done to society itself when corruption persists. Seeing how public officials are quick to take bribes, citizens assume the way to get anything done is the payoff. Inevitably, it tears the social fabric and weakens the sense of community. Cynicism rots the human spirit like an acid rain. Maybe profit *should* come before people? Do rules exist only to be broken?

When we look at all that can go wrong in politics, we need to remember that much goes wrong in every other sphere of human activity. Some people will cheat, lie, steal, and abuse their authority in whatever field they operate in. It isn't politics that makes people behave immorally. But, you may ask, what can be done to improve human nature? Will anything ever make moral the chronic wrongdoers? How can we persuade men and women of decent character to seek office in our cities, our states, and our nation? It is said that good government is made by laws, not by people. But what does law mean to the opportunists who seek only personal profit from public office? A great American jurist, Judge Learned Hand, once wrote: "Liberty lies in the hearts of men and women; when it dies there, no Constitution, no law, no court can save it."

Yet change does come, but only when a great many people down below get mad enough to demand it. It happened during the civil rights struggle and the antiwar resistance of the 1960s. If we *want* to make democracy work, we can. . . .

15

TO MAKE
A DIFFERENCE

Americans do get mad about things that upset them, things that go wrong. If an umpire's bum decision in the last game of a World Series robs their team of the series victory, they are outraged. But why isn't that capacity for anger in the world of sport matched by their response to an outrageous mess in government? Political scandals do not arouse great passion. Is that perhaps because the public has become disillusioned after years of such exposures? The corruption of recent years has occurred at a time when fewer and fewer voters go to the polls.

If lack of interest in public affairs and feelings of powerlessness take deep root it may put the United States on the skids. Even in the small towns, it seems to be happening. In Litchfield, New Hampshire, where town meetings began forty years before the American Revolution, 93 percent of the registered voters failed to turn up in a meeting to decide the budget. Participatory democracy—call it do-it-yourself government—is crumbling. The townsfolk are too busy, too tired, or too indifferent to turn out.

Sometimes people don't act politically because they believe they aren't informed enough on the issues. Politicians who don't want to hear their views tell them to let the "experts" decide such tough questions as arms control. Supposedly *they* have the hard facts and the technical knowledge to make the decisions. But responsible citizens won't be bullied or frightened by experts who put them off with "just trust me, I know what's best." They want to decide their own fate by learning enough to make their own decisions.

"Democracy," says the political scientist Benjamin R. Barber, "depends on a noisy, fractious and self-critical politics, which in turn demands an extraordinary degree of civil resilience and public spirit." If "we leave politics to the politicians, what need have we for citizens? But without citizens there is no public domain, no commonweal, no civic responsibility—and so, all too soon, no democracy."

It's easy to criticize politicians. But we ought to examine ourselves, to see ourselves as we are, not as an abstract "the people." We can't blame everybody in public office and excuse ourselves. "We must adopt the habit," wrote Walter Lippmann some forty years ago, "of thinking as plainly about the sovereign people as we do about the politicians they elect. It will not do to think poorly of the politicians and to talk with bated breath about the voters. No more than the kings before them should the people be hedged with divinity. Like all princes and rulers, they are ill served by flattery and adulation."

As though taking that advice, Professor Barber bluntly says:

Americans, without having yet lost their liberty, seem more concerned about enlarging their private sphere of happiness than invigorating the public sphere in which civil freedom flourishes. They confront without a murmur the wholesale privatization of their country, the selling of the public trust into private hands, the transfer of public tasks (prison, hospitals, schools) to private profit groups, the redefinition of public responsibilities (welfare, support for the arts) as private functions. And what remains of the public domain they leave to politicians and bureaucrats. . . .

There are people who disdain political action because they are "sick and tired" of not getting solutions to problems. They cling to the illusion that there is a single "rational" solution to each problem, whether it is domestic or international, capable of satisfying all conflicting interests. Why don't those idiots in Washington see it? They forget that democratic politics is a process for compromise of different views and interests. It is a way to correct mistakes that people are bound to make. It offers the chance to adjust to changing circumstances. It's the best way, and the nonviolent way, for a society to find answers. But it never guarantees in advance that we'll get the right answer. Yes, it's painful to live with doubt and confusion. But who would want the certainties of a Hitler or a Stalin?

History tells us that human vanity and ambition are often stronger than wisdom and principle. We have to

live with the messy realities of the nation's and the world's problems. We do what we can to stretch the limits of the possible. There are many fine examples of people who point the way. They have not lost the sense of "we." They don't protest injustice only when *they* are the victims and remain silent when a neighbor is the victim. They know what being a citizen means.

To be a political activist does not call for giving up the joys of life. The scientist Stephen Jay Gould suggests a balanced view:

We all accept dissonances to make life supportable in a crazy world, to create islands of sense and comfort in a sea of danger. How else can we tolerate any of life's real and immediate pleasures in a world of apartheid, AIDS, and threat of a nuclear annihilation? Be thankful for this guide of sanity, but beware of the complacency that flows too easily from its comfort.

Feeling good, of course, is not enough. The first six years of the Reagan administration was an era of feeling good. But those six years were paid for by borrowing against our future. The United States borrowed from the rest of the world almost everything it would loan, mortgaging the next generation's future. During those years of feeling good we did little about America's underlying problems—poverty, jobs, housing, education, the homeless, underinvestment and overconsumption, and research and development dedicated to military, rather than economic needs.

No, instead of soothing but baseless optimism we need public leaders capable of seeing the world the way it is, so we can begin to cope with it. Young people in the schools and colleges, says the economist Amitai Etzioni,

must be taught that their future, which is interwoven with the well-being of the country's economy, is best served not by seeking to make as much money as possible as soon as possible, but by doing something of lasting value. And they must be again taught the joy of getting there by the use of decent means, without inside trading, bribes and other illicit and illegal means.

Evidence mounts that there are young people who are idealistic and want to be active. The "me" generation has not taken over the campus entirely. True, the signals the young listened to in the 1980s had not encouraged an interest in public service, either as volunteer or as professional. But on some campuses new signals are being heard. At Wesleyan, Professor Philip P. Hallie runs a course that year after year draws students. It's called "Ethics in History and Literature," and the readings and discussion emphasize flesh-and-blood people in life-and-death situations. At Bryn Mawr, a seminar on "Social Inequality" tries to open up students to the systematic poverty millions of Americans live with and to stimulate them to imagine alternatives. At Amherst, political theory courses find heavy enrollment among students who care about questions that are at once moral and political.

Even when some students want to be active, there is often no support network. So at Stanford, the university opened a Public Service Center. Under its umbrella, students assist refugees from El Salvador, tutor neighborhood children, work in retirement homes, conduct an East Palo Alto summer academy for underprivileged teenagers, or serve internships in Washington, D.C. At Brown University, Student Outreach is the largest organization on campus. Some student volunteers operate a big-brother, big-sister program for children with cancer. Barnard College students work in a soup kitchen. At Harvard, students in one program serve as advocates for the homeless. At Michigan State, students visit children, the handicapped, and the elderly. At Hunter College, students work in the offices of members of the state assembly, in neighborhood associations, and in other agencies as part of an academic program designed to attract them to careers in public service.

While the campus sees a spreading pattern of public service, only a minority of the students are involved thus far. But the college years are an ideal time to develop an interest in community service. It's cultivating "habits of the heart," as one college president said. A senior at Stanford, Jean Kayser, worked in nursing homes and for a Vietnam veterans project in Washington. She was the philanthropy chair for her sorority. She sees it this way: "It is so easy to get caught up in the non-real-world environment of school where you're surrounded by the same kind of people, of the same age, doing the same kind of things. It's important to get out in the real world, to help others who are less fortunate." She co-chaired a campus conference, "You Can Make a Difference," which brought students and faculty together to discuss homelessness, divorce, poverty, day care, and other family issues.

Perhaps young people like Jean Kayser will help turn around the sorry fact that in 1984 only 17 percent of those aged eighteen to twenty-four voted and in 1986 only 7 percent did. Many young people such as Jean Kayser show a growing revulsion from the cynicism that often dominates political life and show a yearning for a climate of greater justice. William J. Brennan, associate justice of the Supreme Court and its senior member, spoke for them and to them in his 1987 commencement address at the Ohio State law school. He criticized "large segments of our population who would keep the country's problems out of sight," and went on to say:

Past legislation and decisions have hardly begun to eliminate the legal inequities in our society. Certainly we as lawyers know the difference between formal and real equality, and therefore we must lead the fight to close the gap between the two. Legislation to date has had little more than formal value because quite frankly it has cost us, the establishment, almost nothing.

Real equality will cost us something. For example, are we willing to pay the substantially higher taxes necessary to make up for past legal deprivations and create a truly just and equitable society? Are we willing to permit public housing or rent subsidy in our neighborhoods? Are we willing to let our sons bear the same risk in time of war as the sons of the poor and the deprived? If not, all our good works in legal assistance programs, public defender offices and the like are meaningless tinkerings which do little more than salve our own consciences.

Are there public officials out there in the city halls, the state houses, and Washington who make a difference and citizens working with them who contribute to that difference? You can find them almost everywhere, if you look. Take Westchester County, just north of New York City. There Paul Feiner, a young county legislator, has a reputation as a longtime activist. In the ninth grade he joined his first volunteer committee. At twenty he played a key role in opening a local political club to women. At twenty-five, after fighting for better public transportation, he ran his own bus service from his parents' home. In 1984 he was elected to office.

As a part-time legislator, Feiner is busy enough for a man with six jobs. This Democrat keeps proposing lots of laws, even though only a few get anywhere in a Republican-controlled legislature. With no paid staff, he set up a student volunteer intern program and often has fifteen young people helping him. Three times a week he sets up his chair and table beside the checkout counters of the big supermarket chain stores and tapes up over his booth his "Problem Solver" sign. He tackles all kinds of queries and pleas for help: supplies bus schedules, lists recreation places, gives tips on low-price fuel, tells where to get low-interest credit cards. He raises money to pay for a child's organ transplant, prevents evictions, finds apartments, and starts a "Have a Heart for the Homeless" fund. His home phone is listed and he encourages calls up to midnight. When he was elected, he quit practicing law, though his salary as a part-timer is only $24,000 a year. At thirty, he said he felt as optimistic about what government can do to help people as he did at twenty.

Another kind of civic reformer was Paul DuBrul, honored by the City University of New York as "an activist, a writer, and an advisor to government leaders." He was cited as one who "championed the cause of the powerless and fought for more equitable distribution of power." He proved, said the *New York Times,* that "one angry person can move government and leave a legacy that will endure even if its inspirer remains largely unsung."

DuBrul, the son of a laborer, grew up Irish in Queens, a borough of New York City. He went to Catholic schools and graduated from Hunter College in 1959. He spoke of himself as a "democratic radical" who believed that only democratic means can bring about lasting change. When he worked for the University Settlement on the Lower East Side he dramatized the tragedy of ghetto children poisoned by tasting the lead paint peeling off tenement walls. He lobbied successfully for a state law that banned the use of lead paint in apartments.

DuBrul began as a journalist in the muckraking tradition of Lincoln Steffens, but he soon decided that exposing wrongs wasn't enough. So he became an organizer of action—for labor unions, for civil rights groups, and for the poor in urban ghettos. Then, having seen how much needed to be done, he went directly into politics and was appointed special assistant to the Social Services Commissioner of New York State. He suffered from cystic fibrosis from childhood on, surviving the crippling disease far longer than is common. Asked how he managed to cope with his illness, DuBrul said, by balancing rage and humor, because "if you spend a lot of time saying 'why me?' you'll find out too soon." In 1987, at the age of forty-nine, he died.

Another example is Robert M. Hayes, who has fought the cause of the homeless in New York City. What he has done is a model for all those others trying to help the 2 to 3 million people in the United States who have no place to call home. They are people in trouble, trying to survive under bridges, in doorways, beside boxcars, in parks, tents, emergency shelters, subways, and abandoned cars. Among them are abused wives and cast-off children, evicted families, and lonely old people. They are a part of the 35 to 50 million Americans who are poor.

Hayes was a young lawyer when he was first moved to try to help the homeless. It began when he talked one day to men living on the street near his home in Manhattan. He asked them why they did not go to a shelter, and he learned that the few shelters provided were dirty, dangerous, and overcrowded. Hayes went to city officials to seek action. When he made no progress, he put his legal training to work. He quit his job with a prestigious Wall Street law firm and set up operations in a cheap office in midtown. He had never tried a case, but he filed his first suit on behalf of homeless men needing shelter. And won.

Next Hayes organized a nonprofit Coalition for the Homeless. With a beginning budget of $75,000, it grew in five years to a $1.2-million-a-year program. Foundations pay about half his costs, and government subsidizes the rest. The coalition has brought over a dozen lawsuits, drawing on major law firms for free legal service.

The court actions won the right to shelter for men, then for women, and finally for families. The decisions also helped improve conditions for boarder babies and for older children about to leave for foster care. Gradually the coalition reached out to make improvements in a wider range of human needs: standards for the city's foster care system, the handling of the mentally ill, and the treatment of AIDS patients.

Working outside the political system, Hayes has learned how to bring about social change. One: do enough preaching for people to care. Two: then get something real done, like a piece of legislation or a court order. And three: keep plugging away at it. If nothing happens, if a deadline isn't met, sue. He believes the third step is crucial. Too often people don't follow through. The momentum is lost and the interest fades.

By the late 1980s, the coalition, now national, was also running several service programs—a sleepaway summer camp for homeless children, a soup kitchen at Grand Central Terminal, and a lunch program in the rundown hotels where the city houses homeless families. Hayes had raised his sights to Washington, pressuring the federal government to build housing for the poor.

That lawsuits can change politics is a belief strongly held by many other people like Robert Hayes. In a drab row house in sight of the national Capitol is a team of lawyers and investigators who have been making waves with lawsuits ever since 1980. They are members of the Christic Institute led by a husband-and-wife team, Daniel P. Sheehan and Sara Nelson. The institute takes its name from the "Christic force." It is the concept of a Jesuit priest that a harmonious force bands all things together and overpowers human-made destructive forces. Although the institute is not religious, it has a deep faith in its ability to influence public opinion and national policy. Staffed by some thirty-five men and women, mostly young, the Christic Institute has pursued a social-action agenda to victory in many important cases. It won $400,000 in damages from the city of Greensboro, North Carolina, for the families of five people killed at a 1979 demonstration against the Ku Klux Klan. It won a settlement of

$1.38 million in a suit against the Oklahoma-based Kerr-McGee Corporation for the family of Karen Silkwood in a suit involving plutonium contamination at the plant where Silkwood worked. It takes up many social and political issues, such as defense of a woman in Texas charged with violating immigration laws by providing sanctuary to illegal aliens. The nonprofit institute is run as a cooperative with staff living in a group home owned by the institute and all drawing the same low salaries. Support comes from private donations and public-interest and religious groups.

No lawyer, but rather a Pullman porter, E. D. Nixon had his own way of changing politics. He is a man whom most Americans have never heard of. But when he died in 1987, at the same age as the century, he left as his legacy a nation he had helped change radically. In his childhood and for much of his life, black Americans lived under a rigid system of discrimination and segregation. Nixon made his living as a Pullman porter, but his real life's work was winning rights for himself and his people. As a young man, he joined with A. Philip Randolph to organize the Brotherhood of Sleeping Car Porters, the first successful black union. In the 1940s, as head of the Voters League of Alabama, he led 750 black citizens to the county courthouse to demand that they be allowed to vote. In 1954, he lost his campaign for county official of the Democratic party, but he was the first black to seek political office in Montgomery, Alabama, since Reconstruction.

As his courageous actions stirred the civil rights movement to life, E. D. Nixon continued to play an important role that never made the headlines. That day in 1955 when Rosa Parks was arrested for violating the Jim Crow laws by refusing to give up her seat in the white section of the bus, Nixon bailed her out of jail. As head of the Montgomery Improvement Association, he organized the city's blacks for a boycott of the buses and asked the young and unknown preacher, Dr. Martin Luther King, Jr., to lead the protest. "I knew then that something could be done," Nixon said long after. He had a great hand in getting it done.

The private effort to provide free meals for the hungry is perhaps the best example of the triumph of civic spirit. Back in 1982 about 30 organizations did this in New York City; five years later there were almost 500. One of these is the Neighbors Together Soup Kitchen, directed by Sister Lillian Graziano. When it opened its doors, it served 75 meals a week, and five years later the organization was serving 350 meals each day. It's not that the people who come in are homeless, said Sister Lillian Graziano. Some are, but many more are from low-income families, who run out of money, defeated by the cost of rent and utilities.

Some volunteers in this national effort to meet an emergency can't help but wonder if it's the right thing they are doing. By dealing privately with what is a social problem, are they making it easier for government to do less? To duck its human responsibility? Or are they simply recognizing the brute fact that government is failing to provide for the basic needs of its citizens?

Most cities now see both forces operating—the private and the governmental. In New York, for example, the city set up an Office of Food Policy Coordination with a budget of a few million dollars. Chosen to head it was Pamela W. Green, who for four years had directed a food bank in the Bronx. She had solicited donations of surplus food from manufacturers and retailers and distributed them to soup kitchens and pantries. In one year alone her group gave out 4 million pounds of food. By 1987, volunteer groups were serving a million meals a month to New York's hungry people.

It's not only the well-off remembering those who are not. "It's the poor taking care of the poor," said Green. One woman in her Bronx neighborhood fed 200 people a week out of her own social security check. "When a bill would come, she would tell me, 'The Lord will provide.' She was saying that the day she died."

But Green thinks it's shortsighted to consider voluntary action a solution. "Folks have a limit," she said. "What if all these people one day burn out?" She hopes more people, helping as volunteers, will come to understand their own vulnerability and realize they should vote for politicians who will increase federal benefits. Many of us in the middle class are only one paycheck away from being homeless. "If we don't vote to take care of the problem," she said, "we'll be the next in line."

When she took the job, Pamela Green worried about crossing the line between people's advocate and public bureaucrat. She didn't want to wake up and find that the people she had been working with were now throwing stones at her. But that's a risk activists must sometimes take. A Catholic priest, Monsignor Geno C. Baroni, knew that and lived it. Monsignor Baroni, the pastor of a neighborhood church in a largely black district of Washington,

D.C., was known for many years as a fighter for social justice. Back in 1970 he had organized a conference in the capital to bring about a community alliance among whites, blacks and other minorities, and blue- and white-collar workers. He urged community leaders to think about running for office. "Get inside the doors," he said.

One of the people at that meeting was Barbara Mikulski. She listened and traded her picket signs for bumper stickers. She was elected to the House of Representatives from Maryland and now is a U.S. senator and an ardent voice for human needs and rights. Monsignor Baroni later took his own advice and accepted an appointment as assistant secretary of the Department of Housing and Urban Development (HUD). When he died of cancer at fifty-three, neighborhood organizers nationwide recognized what he had done both as agitator and public official. "He was able to be a voice inside the policymaking forum," said Joe McNeely of Baltimore, "and while it didn't have the distinctiveness of when he was outside leading the march, he created his own turmoil at HUD by insisting that certain values be incorporated into the HUD policy—was HUD just there to promote real-estate expansion or to provide shelter for poor people?"

When a Baroni Society was formed to honor the priest and carry on his work, its president said that Monsignor Baroni knew that "bureaucracy is people. . . . He became a bureaucrat because he knew the only change in bureaucracy comes through a change in the people."

A Barbara Mikulski and a Pamela Green show how real a future there is for women in politics. The governor of Vermont, Madeleine M. Kunin, came to the United

States as a child at the outbreak of World War II. Knowing the legacy of the Holocaust, she learned at an early age that "essentially we are responsible for our lives. Passivity provides no protection." Political courage, she told a convention of the National Political Women's Caucus,

stems from a number of causes: anger, pain, love, hate. There is no lack of political motivation within women. We feel it all. Anger at a world which rushes toward saber-rattling displays of power. Pain at a world which ignores the suffering of its homeless, its elderly, its children. Hatred towards the injustice which occurs daily as the strong overpower the weak. And love for the dream of peace on earth.

All this and much more is within us to express. That is the first step toward political self-realization. It's back to basics: first you have to want to change the world, then you find a way to do it. . . .

In Governor Kunin's own case, she started with a strong desire to have an effect upon events around her. For her it was a flashing red light needed at the railroad crossing in her neighborhood to protect her children on their walk to school. Her success in obtaining the flashing red signal as a private citizen led step-by-step to her ability to improve Vermont's environmental laws as governor. "Each step builds a new self-image, enabling us to move from the passive to the active voice."

She urged women not to suppress their own personal values when they recognize that they are in direct conflict with how the real world operates. Live a life where you transform your personal values into public action, she said. You'll see real change take place—better schools, clean water, welfare reform, a nuclear disarmament treaty. . . . She calls it "a marvelous privilege to be in public life," to refuse to accept any split between being in charge and being feminine. "Our goal is to humanize this world by combining both; let us begin."

Millions have already begun. In every community you can see a generous spirit at work. One of every four Americans does some kind of unpaid volunteer work. And this despite the talk about the individualism that strives to get what it wants for itself, paying no heed to the needs of others. The 1980s supplied ample evidence of meanness in business and politics, but there is evidence on the other side, too. Most people want to live by humane, not selfish values. They believe that having close friends and a good family life is more important than making a lot of money and beating out everyone else.

A Gallup survey in the 1980s found young Americans to be less self-centered than supposed. They want to be of service or help to others. The willingness is there; what's needed sometimes is the outlet for that desire. If to be free and prosperous is the nation's goal, then perhaps the way to realize that goal for all Americans is to make our political democracy serve human ends.

A NOTE
ON SOURCES

Anyone of voting age who sets out to write a book about politics knows at least a little about it. Partly from schoolbooks, something perhaps from family, and maybe a little from personal experience. In my case, personal experience goes back a long way. My first vote was cast for Franklin D. Roosevelt in 1936. I was twenty-one and clinging tenaciously to my new job on the Federal Theater Project in New York. It was part of a vast work relief program for those millions of jobless and hungry Americans in the Great Depression. The WPA, as it was called, was open to people in need who did almost anything—ditch diggers, plumbers, secretaries, teachers, sales people, clerks, nurses — and also open to writers, artists, actors, and musicians forced to go on relief. Art, like bridges, schools, roads, dams, was a necessity, FDR said, something everybody's spirit thirsted for. His administration had gotten the money from Congress to support this radically new idea, and I gladly cast my ballot for him in the hope he would continue the program. A first lesson in politics: he did something for us needy ones; now we would do something for him (and of course for ourselves at the same time).

The lessons kept coming. Congress wasn't wild about giving money to people in the arts. Not back then, and not even when it meant feeding us or letting us starve. They were nervous about writers and painters and musicians and actors. Oddballs: who knew what they would do next? So the budget for the WPA arts projects was always at risk. Congress slashed the funds and thousands of us were laid off. Again and again. I learned lesson number two: You have to fight for what you need. I found myself on picket lines to protest cuts and demand adequate appropriations. We picketed on the streets of New York, and we rode by bus south to Washington to picket the Capitol, too. Not once, but many times. We even borrowed an idea from the striking auto workers in Michigan by using sit-downs and work stoppages inside the project offices to get media attention and enlist public support.

A third lesson came when our picket line was sometimes roughed up by the cops or they threw us down a flight of stairs to get us out of project headquarters. Protest—even our nonviolent sort—is a challenge to those in authority who prefer order to free speech. They often end up using violence to secure order.

But I had an even earlier start in political action. (You don't have to wait till you're old enough to vote.) As a student at Columbia, I carried placards in peace demonstrations both on and off the campus. This was in the early 1930s when a student movement had sprung up on campuses all over the country dedicated to pressuring the president and Congress to work for peace. We joined women's groups and the clergy in a series of "No More War" parades. The folly of World War I had burned into our generation's mind, and many Americans backed steps taken toward disarmament. In the spring of 1935, sixty thousand college students went on a nationwide strike against war.

It didn't work that time. World War II exploded in our faces. But now, because it was a war against Hitlerism, against fascism, I too put on a uniform. Sometimes politics fails and force takes over. Hitlers aren't interested in political compromise.

Later, after the war, I worked for a trade union that tried, and failed, to stop Congress from passing an anti-labor law that seriously restricted the right of working people to organize to improve their conditions. Then I joined the staff of the former vice president, Henry A. Wallace, when he ran unsuccessfully for president on a third-party ticket.

In a long life there have been many political lessons to learn. This is the first time, however, that I've tried to make sense out of it for a book. I thought I knew a fair amount before I began research, but I found rich resources that deepened my understanding. The literature of politics is immense. Since this was intended to be a short book, I could not embrace everything nor go into anything in great detail. I hoped to provide enough background on the beginnings of our political system so that readers may see where it all comes from and then to focus on the political events and developments of more recent times. This was done so that readers may have a clearer sense of where we are now and where we might go in the future.

My sources are quite varied. They include, first of all, the many scholarly studies cited in the Bibliography: books, periodicals, special reports. I might point out how exhaustive the references are. Oleszek's book on congressional procedures, for example, has 200 references dealing with that subject alone. Then there are autobiographies and biographies describing what political figures have done and offering perhaps some insight into why they did it. For those with a keen appetite for politics and politicians, there are a great many books addressed to the general reader. They take up political events, trends, periods, personalities, machines, parties, and the like. The Oral History projects of several universities have taped the memoirs of hundreds of political figures, most of them accessible in typescript. I've also made use of political newsletters, from those issued by legislators for their constituents, to the "insider" publications by less biased observers of the political scene. The press in many major cities is, of course, a basic source. I owe a great debt to the *New York Times* for its daily reporting on politics. My file of clippings from its pages proved to be full of the rich detail one needs to bring the story alive. Other papers such as the *Washington Post,* the *Los Angeles Times,* and the *Baltimore Sun* would serve the same purpose. I am also thankful for the frequent political pieces of the *New Yorker* magazine, especially those by Elizabeth Drew and Andy Logan.

Finally, I am an old fan of the weekly TV program "Washington Week in Review" heard over the Public Broadcasting System. To Paul Duke and his assembly of fine reporters, my deepest thanks for many enlightening half hours.

BIBLIOGRAPHY

Asbell, Bernard. *The Senate Nobody Knows*. Baltimore: Johns Hopkins University Press, 1978.

Bagdikian, Ben. *The Media Monopoly*. Boston: Beacon, 1983.

Blume, Keith. *The Presidential Election Show*. South Hadley: Bergin and Garvey, 1985.

Bollet, Paul F., Jr. *Presidential Campaigns*. New York: Oxford University Press, 1984.

Boyte, Harry C. *Citizen Action and the New American Populism*. Philadelphia: Temple University Press, 1986.

Browne, Arthur. *I, Koch*. New York: Dodd, Mead, 1985.

Caro, Robert. *The Power Broker*. New York: Knopf, 1974.

Crick, Bernard. *In Defense of Politics*. New York: Penguin, 1982.

Diggins, John P. *The Lost Soul of American Politics*. New York: Basic, 1984.

Edsall, Thomas B. *The New Politics of Inequality*. New York: Norton, 1984.

Gallup Organization. *The People, Press & Politics*. Los Angeles: Times Mirror, 1987.

Green, Mark, and Michael Calabrese. *Who Runs Congress?* New York: Bantam, 1979.

Hofstadter, Richard. *The American Political Tradition.* New York: Knopf, 1948.

Hofstadter, Richard, ed. *The Progressive Movement 1900–1915.* Englewood Cliffs: Prentice-Hall, 1963.

Hughes, Emmet John. *The Ordeal of Power.* New York: Atheneum, 1962.

Hummel, Ralph P., and Robert A. Isaak. *The Real American Politics.* Englewood Cliffs: Prentice-Hall, 1986.

"In Search of New York." *Dissent,* Special Issue, Fall, 1987.

Kelman, Steven. *Making Public Policy: A Hopeful View of American Government.* New York: Basic, 1987.

Key, V. O. *Politics, Parties and Pressure Groups.* New York: Crowell, 1946.

LaPalombara, Joseph, and Myron Weiner, eds. *Political Parties and Political Development.* Princeton: Princeton University Press, 1966.

Lekachman, Robert. *Greed Is Not Enough: Reaganomics.* New York: Pantheon, 1982.

Lubell, Samuel. *The Future of American Politics.* Garden City: Doubleday, 1956.

McCormick, Richard P. *The Presidential Game: The Origins of American Presidential Politics.* New York: Oxford, 1982.

McGinniss, Joe. *The Selling of the President, 1968.* New York: Pocket, 1969.

Miller, James A. *Running in Place: Inside the Senate.* New York: Touchstone, 1987.

Nelson, William N. *On Justifying Democracy.* Boston: Routledge & Kegan Paul, 1980.

Neustadt, Richard E. *Presidential Power.* New York: Wiley, 1960.

Nicholas, H. G. *The Nature of American Politics.* New York: Oxford University Press, 1986.

Oleszek, Walter J. *Congressional Procedures and the Policy Process*. Washington: Congressional Quarterly Press, 1978.

Parenti, Michael. *Democracy for the Few*. New York: St. Martin's, 1983.

Peavey, Fran. *Heart Politics*. Philadelphia: New Society, 1986.

Polsby, Nelson W., and Aaron Wildavsky. *Presidential Elections*. New York: Scribner's, 1976.

Raskin, Marcus G. *The Common Good: Its Politics, Policies and Philosophy*. New York: Routledge & Kegan Paul, 1986.

Reedy, George E. *The Twilight of the Presidency*. New York: New American Library, 1970.

————. *The U.S. Senate: Paralysis or a Search for Consensus?* New York: Crown, 1986.

Roseboom, Eugene H. *A History of Presidential Elections*. New York: Macmillan, 1957.

Rossiter, Clinton. *Parties and Politics in America*. Ithaca: Cornell University Press, 1960.

Royko, Mike. *Boss: Richard Daley of Chicago*. New York: Dutton, 1971.

Seidman, Harold, and Robert Gilmour. *Politics, Position, and Power*. New York: Oxford University Press, 1986.

Sherrill, Robert. *Why They Call It Politics: A Guide to America's Government*. New York: Harcourt Brace Jovanovich, 1974.

Shogan, Robert. *None of the Above: Why Presidents Fail and What Can Be Done About It*. New York: Mentor, 1983.

Smith, Hedrick. *The Power Game: How Washington Really Works*. New York: Random House, 1988.

Tebbel, John, and Sarah Watts. *The Press and the Presidency: From George Washington to Ronald Reagan*. New York: Oxford, 1985.

Warren, Sidney, ed. *The American President*. Englewood Cliffs: Prentice-Hall, 1967.

INDEX

AIDS, 112, 156, 162
Alabama, 164
Alaska, 138
Albany, N.Y., 140
American Israel Public Affairs Committee (AIPAC), 110–11
American Revolution, 12, 152
Amherst College, 157
Articles of Confederation, 9, 68
Asseltine, James K., 122

Bailey, Stephen, 82
Baker, Russell, 48–50
Barber, Benjamin, 153–54
Baroni, Gene, 166–67
Biaggi, Mario, 115
Bill of Rights, 17, 18–20

blacks, 24, 63, 98–99, 133, 164–65
Bork, Robert, 104
Boston, 42, 146
Brandeis, Louis, 98, 101, 103
Brennan, William, 159
bribery, 38–42, 94, 105, 115–16, 130–31, 138, 140–41, 157
Brown, Marshall, 149
Brown University, 158
Bryn Mawr College, 157
Buchanan, James, 84
bureaucracy, 118–27
Bush, George, 7
business, influence of, 130–31, 136, 138–39, 146, 148–49, 157

Calhoun, John C., 96
Caplan, Lincoln, 102, 105
Catholics, 20
checks and balances, 16–
17, 68
Chicago, 34, 138, 142, 146
child care, 92–93
China, 61
Christic Institute, 163–64
civil disobedience, 24
civil rights, 21, 136, 137,
151, 161, 164–65
Civil War, 129, 130
Clay, Henry, 96
Coalition for the Homeless,
162–63
coalitions, 62–63
Colfax, Schuyler, 38
Committee for Study of the
American Electorate, 53,
54
Common Cause, 42
Congress, 15, 17, 71, 80–
96, 109, 111, 113, 118,
122, 124, 125, 126
Constitution, U.S., 9, 80–
81, 97
Constitutional law, 12–18,
68–69, 80, 129
Continental Congress, 9
Corrupt practices acts, 135
corruption, 8, 25, 35–42,
51, 152
Cox, James, 134
Cranston, Alan, 39

Daley, Richard, 34, 136,
138

Dallas Times Herald, 41
D'Amato, Alfonse, 39
Declaration of Indepen-
dence, 21
Defense Department, 118
democracy, 3, 153
Democratic party, 7, 28–
29, 62–66, 143, 145
Des Moines Register, 41
direct primary, 134
Discher, Lewis, 138
Dred Scott v. Sandford
decision, 99
Drew, Elizabeth, 35–36
Dubrow, Evelyn, 111
DuBrul, Paul, 160–61
Dukakis, Michael, 7

education, 2, 58, 157–58
Edwards, Mickey, 93
Eisenhower, Dwight, 50,
63, 72
elections, 7, 32–33, 34, 43–
60
environment, 89, 107, 136
equality, 159
ethics, 139, 157
Etzioni, Amitai, 157

fascism, 31, 172
federal agencies, 118–27
Federal Communications
Commission, 56
Federal Elections Commis-
sion, 45
Federalists, 25–26
Feiner, Paul, 159
Fitzgerald, Ernest, 124

Ford, Gerald, 63
Fortune, 110
Frankfurter, Felix, 102
Franklin, Benjamin, 6–7, 9, 13, 20
Friedman, Stanley, 143, 146, 147
Frost, David, 75
Full Employment Act, 82
fund raising, 34–42, 64–65

Gans, Curtis, 53
Garfield, James, 38
Georgia, 140
Gerry, Elbridge, 13
Giuliani, Rudolph, 143, 146
Gould, Stephen Jay, 156
Grace Commission, 126
Graziano, Lillian, 165
Great Depression, 62
Green, Mark, 39
Green, Pamela, 166, 167
Gulf Oil, 116

Hague, Frank, 136
Hallie, Philip P., 157
Hamilton, Alexander, 14, 25
Hand, Learned, 102, 150
Harlan, John, 102
Harris, Richard, 39
Harvard University, 158
Hayes, Robert, 161–63
health insurance, 64
Helmsley, Harry, 148
high-tech campaigns, 7, 43–51
Hitler, Adolf, 154

Hofstadter, Richard, 130
homeless, 161–63
"horse trading," 91
House of Representatives, 40–41, 80–96
housing, 64, 159, 163
Hughes, Charles Evans, 101, 134
Hughes, Howard, 116
hunger, 165–66
Hunter College, 158, 161

income spread, 65
influence peddling, 94
Iran-Contra affair, 75–76, 105

Jackson, Andrew, 28
Javits, Jacob, 112
Jefferson, Thomas, 20, 25, 26
Jews, 20, 44
jobs, 64
Johnson, Hiram, 134
Johnson, Lyndon, 77, 78, 89

Kayser, Jean, 158
Key, V. O., 29, 58
King, Martin Luther, 165
Kissinger, Henry, 73
Koch, Edward, 145, 148, 149
Korean War, 81, 89
Kotz, David M., 136
Ku Klux Klan, 163
Kunin, Madeleine, 167–69

La Follette, Robert M., 134
Lasswell, Harold, 109
law-making process, 82–95
Lincoln, Abraham, 28, 71, 101
Lincoln-Douglas debates, 33
Lippmann, Walter, 153
lobbyists, 65, 107–17, 121, 138
"logrolling," 94
Long, Russell, 39

McNeely, Joe, 167
Madison, James, 13, 14
Magna Carta, 18
maldistribution of wealth, 135–36
Manes, Donald, 143, 144, 147
Marbury v. Madison, 99
Marshall, John, 99
Marshall, Thurgood, 101
Mason, George, 18
media, 7–8, 47–51, 58–59
Meese, Edwin, 104–05, 115
Michigan State University, 158
Mikulski, Barbara, 167
military juntas, 31
military spending, 92, 115, 124, 126, 137
Miller, Samuel, 101
minority rights, 17
Missouri Compromise, 99
Mondale, Walter, 48
muckrakers, 133, 138

Muller v. Oregon, 98
multiparty systems, 61

Nader, Ralph, 56
Nelson, Sara, 163
New York City, 142–49, 161–63, 165–66
New York Daily News, 145
New York State, 139–41
New York Times, 110, 115, 140, 146
New Yorker, 39, 105
Newfield, Jack, 146, 147
Nicaragua, 75
Nixon, E. D., 164–65
Nixon, Richard, 63, 71, 74–75, 78, 89, 105
Nuclear Regulatory Commission (NRC), 122

Occupational Safety and Health Administration (OSHA), 121–22
Oklahoma, 140, 164
oligarchy, 3
ombudsman, 95
O'Neill, Thomas ("Tip"), 116
one-party states, 61
opinion polls, 46–47

Parks, Rosa, 165
party bosses, 33–34, 130–31, 136, 147
party membership, 62
patronage, 149–50
Philadelphia, 142, 143, 146
Plessy v. Ferguson, 98

political action committees (PACs), 40–42, 64, 65, 109
political activists, 156–69
political advertising, 44, 47, 54–57
political bosses, 33–34, 130–31, 136, 147
political management, 43–51
political parties, 30, 33, 61–66, 130–31, 136, 146, 147, 148–50
political polls, 46–47
politics, art of, 1–7; and bureaucracy, 121; as compromise, 4, 23, 154; and corruption, 142–51; defined, 4, 21; diversity the root of, 30; economic issues in, 2, 23; high-tech aspect of, 43–51; and influence of business on, 130–31, 136; as mixture of self-interest and public interest, 6, 7; origins of, 2–3; revolution or civil war as alternatives to, 24
pollution, 2
poor people, 64, 92, 125–26, 129, 136, 161–63, 165–67
Postal Service, 118
power, abuses of, 4–5, 105, 113; of business, 130–31; of city machines, 146; defined, 24; lacked by poor, 124–26; of railroads, 131; of real estate developers, 148–50; resources for, 24; and wealth, 135–36
presidents: burdens of, 79; and Congress, 71, 73–74; isolation of, 77–78; role of, 16, 68–79; and Supreme Court, 105; types of, 69
pressure groups, 107–17
primaries, 34, 66
Progressives, 133–36
property, distribution of, 10
Protestants, 62
public authorities, 141
public domain, 154
public policy, 23, 104
public works, 64

Rabb, Selwyn, 146
racism, 6
Randolph, A. Philip, 164
Reagan, Ronald, 46, 51, 52, 56–57, 75, 78, 89, 92, 104, 105, 113, 121, 136–37, 156
Reedy, George, 77–79, 91
reform movements, 66, 133–36, 148
Republican party, 7, 28–29, 45, 46, 62–66, 148
Reston, James, 7
Robbins, Liz, 112
Rogers, Will, 41
Roosevelt, Franklin, 62, 170
Rosenblum, Herb, 125
Royko, Mike, 138

Senate, 39–41, 80–96, 124, 135
Seventeenth Amendment, 17, 135
sexism, 6
Shays's Rebellion, 12–13
Sheehan, Daniel P., 163
Sherman, Roger, 14
Silkwood, Karen, 164
Simon, Stanley, 115
Sinclair, Upton, 138
slavery, 15, 17, 33
Smith, Adam, 10
social change, steps to, 162–63
Social security, 23, 64
Soviet Union, 61
"special interests," 107–17
Stalin, Joseph, 154
Stanford University, 157, 158
state government, 128–41, 148
states' rights, 137
Steffens, Lincoln, 138, 161
Supreme Court: class bias of, 101; and desegregation, 98–101; functions of, 16, 97–106; and innovation, 101; and "judicial restraint," 102; and original intent, 99; "packing of," 103; political influence on, 103
Syracuse, 142, 143

Tarbell, Ida, 138
taxation, 2, 23, 64, 149, 159

Teapot Dome scandal, 113
television campaigning, 7–8, 32, 44, 47, 48, 50, 54–57
third parties, 28–29
Thruway Authority, 141
Time, 113
totalitarianism, 3
Truman, Harry S., 72, 89
Trump, Donald, 148
Twain, Mark, 38
Tweed, William, 136
two-party system, 26–29, 61–66
tyranny, 3

USA Today, 75

Veterans Administration, 118
Vietnam War, 81, 89
voluntary action, 157–69
voter participation, 8, 52–59
voting: effect of TV on, 7–8, 54, 56, 57; in elections of 1942, 52; 1960, 52, 53; 1980, 53, 59; 1986, 52, 56, 63, 96; 1988, 7–8; by "independents," 59–60; patterns in, 53; reasons for low turnout, 7, 52–59; trends away from, 52–60
Voting Rights Act, 63

War Powers Act, 81
Warren, Earl, 98
Washington, D.C., 142, 163
Washington, George, 14, 25, 26, 69, 118
Washington Post, 41, 105
Watergate crisis, 61, 74, 76, 113
wealth, in U.S., 135–36
Webster, Daniel, 96
Wedtech scandal, 105, 115
welfare, 23, 136
Wesleyan University, 157
whistle-blowers, 118, 124–25, 148

White, William Allen, 130–131
Wild, Claude, Jr., 116
Wilson, Woodrow, 103, 134, 135
women, 10, 17, 133, 163–69
World War II, 72, 94, 96

young activists, 157–60

Zimmerman, William, 58
Zornow, David, 147
Zschau, Ed, 39